CW00689246

The Art of
CALLIGRAPHY
in Modern China

The Art of
CALLIGRAPHY
in Modern China

Gordon S. Barrass

THE BRITISH MUSEUM PRESS

For Kristen

© 2002 Gordon S. Barrass

First published in 2002 by
The British Museum Press
A division of The British Museum Company Ltd
46 Bloomsbury Street, London WC1B 3QQ

Gordon S. Barrass has asserted the moral right
to be identified as the author of this work

A catalogue record for this book is available
from the British Library

ISBN 0 7141 2400 1

Designed by Gillian Greenwood
Typeset in Joanna and Photina by Helen Robertson
Printed in Italy by L.E.G.O. SpA

CONTENTS

FOREWORD

The British Museum became increasingly interested during the 1980s in the development of calligraphy in modern China. In 1993 we invited Gordon Barrass to help us create a collection covering the period from the founding of The People's Republic of China in 1949 through to the present.

Gordon had been keenly interested in Chinese culture for many years. While serving in the British Embassy in Beijing from 1970–72, he collected some very interesting pieces of nineteenth- and twentieth-century Chinese calligraphy. In 1973 he was the joint head of the Anglo-French delegation that negotiated the arrangements for the famous 'Chinese Exhibition' of recently discovered archaeological treasures to travel from Beijing, first to Paris and London (where it was held at the Royal Academy in 1973–4) and then on to several other countries.

Since Gordon left the Diplomatic Service in 1993 to become the International Advisor to Coopers & Lybrand (later PriceWaterhouseCoopers), he has made more than fifty visits to China. There he managed to meet many leading calligraphers, as well as the relatives or friends of famous calligraphers who were no longer alive.

Over the past eight years he has collected a fascinating range of material and persuaded many leading calligraphers to donate works to the Museum. I would like to take this opportunity to thank our Chinese friends once again for their generosity. The details of their donations are given on page 274.

This book is published to accompany an exhibition at The British Museum, which contains many pieces from our new collection. I believe its lucid style and beautiful illustrations will help introduce the delights of calligraphy – both modern and classical – to a wider and non-specialist audience.

The Museum is very grateful to Gordon Barrass himself for so generously donating his collection of calligraphy to The British Museum. This has greatly enhanced its holdings of such material. The foresight and energy he has displayed in collating this collection has enormously benefited The British Museum, so that it may now be considered to possess a world-class collection of modern Chinese calligraphy.

GRAHAM C. GREENE
CHAIRMAN OF THE TRUSTEES OF THE BRITISH MUSEUM

德國海因利希·伯爾遺作〈用這雙手〉的幾句

一九九二年 郭大鋒譯當子以商周文字書之

ACKNOWLEDGEMENTS

I wish to thank each of the contemporary artists about whom I have written here, not only for helping me to understand their own work but also for providing valuable insights into the work of leading calligraphers who are now dead, and into the way calligraphy has developed in China since 1949. They have all been most generous with their time and patient in their explanations. I am similarly indebted to Chen Haosu and Guo Pingying for helping me to understand the works of their respective fathers, Marshal Chen Yi and Guo Moruo.

Several leading experts in Chinese culture and politics have kindly assisted me with my research and commented on the text: Dr Bai Qianshen, Prof. Richard Barnhart, Prof. Cao Yiqiang, Prof. Glen Dudbridge, Dr Anne Farrer, H. E. Geng Biao, Dr Geng Yan, Prof. Hu Yunhuan, Prof. Lo Ch'ing, Prof. Roderick MacFarquhar, Jonathan Mirsky, Qian Ning, H. E. Wang Daohan, Dr Wang Tao, James C. Y. Watt, Prof. Roderick Whitfield, Harold Wong, Dr Frances Wood, Yang Xianyi and Yang Yingshi.

I am particularly indebted to Dr Alison Hardie for her unstinting help in the final preparation of the book. She provided valuable additional information for some of the biographical sketches, reviewed and polished the translations, transcribed the calligraphy into printed Chinese characters and prepared the Chinese bibliography. Her wide-ranging knowledge of Chinese history and culture greatly facilitated my efforts to set the developments of the past half-century into perspective.

Throughout this project I have had the warmest possible support from The British Museum – in particular, Graham Greene, the Chairman of the Board of Trustees; Dr Robert Anderson, the Director; Dr Jessica Rawson, former Keeper of Oriental Antiquities, who first suggested this project to me; Robert Knox, the present Keeper, who has been so helpful with the preparation of this book, and his colleagues Mary Ginsberg, Carol Michaelson and Jane Portal, as well as John Williams and Kevin Lovelock of the Department of Photography and Imaging.

I am grateful to The British Museum Press for providing me with an excellent editor, Nina Shandloff, and a talented designer, Gillian Greenwood, who have been most ably assisted by Susanne Atkin, Bill Jones, Susan Leiper, Richard Mason and Helen Robertson.

No one has given me greater encouragement and support than my wife, Kristen Lippincott, who has been my muse throughout this project. Not only did she bring her keen mind and experienced eye to bear on the complex issues of modern calligraphy and how these could best be explained to a non-specialist audience, she did so with a tact that would have been deeply appreciated by any author, especially a spouse.

INTRODUCTION

Had I been born Chinese, I would have been a calligrapher, not a painter.
PABLO PICASSO

Although many societies have a tradition of creating beautiful calligraphy, few can rival what the Chinese have achieved with their splendid brushes, inks and papers. For millennia, calligraphy has been a defining feature of Chinese culture and one of its most revered forms of art. Sadly, most Westerners find Chinese calligraphy difficult to understand. However, recently a new window has been opened on the subject. From the extraordinary upheavals and reforms in China during the past fifty years, calligraphy has re-emerged with a new vitality. It is now attracting the interest of a much wider international circle of people, most of whom are unable to read Chinese.

Calligraphers have always used their art to lend weight and beauty to the message they are conveying. The calligraphy of the modern period is more approachable for Westerners as a result of changes in both Western and Chinese aesthetics. In particular, developments in Western abstract art and the increasing influence that Western art has had on many Chinese calligraphers have helped narrow the gap in artistic taste.

The content, too, is easier to understand. Calligraphy has become a livelier vehicle for personal expression, with feelings being conveyed far more directly than in recent centuries. Many of the people discussed in this book have been involved in the convulsions of Chinese history to a far greater extent than most famous calligraphers of the past. We know much about their lives and often exactly why they wrote what they did.

Over the past half-century four distinct trends have been evident in calligraphy. Initially, by far the most influential of these was the continuation of the 'Grand Tradition' of Classical calligraphy. Then, in the mid-1980s, a Modernist movement emerged that created an entirely new genre of the art. Later, the decline in the number of truly Classical calligraphers was offset by the rise of many younger Neo-Classicists, who keep the Classical ideals alive by setting them within a modern context. More recently still, an Avant-Garde movement has come to the fore, exploring new artistic possibilities by combining calligraphic imagery and techniques with the modern forms of conceptual and performance art.

This book begins by outlining the factors that have shaped the development of calligraphy in China. The first chapter examines the continuing, and often heated, debate over the nature of the art and its future. Because the art is best understood by examining the circumstances from which it emerged, the second chapter explores the influences that have shaped it over the past fifty years.

The greater part of the book is composed of short chapters on twenty-five people who have been key figures in the development of the art of calligraphy or whose work illustrates some of its trends. I have concentrated on individual artists rather than on styles, because I believe that by understanding their lives it becomes easier to appreciate their art – and the artists themselves are often highly articulate about what they are trying to do.

In China the *cognoscenti* broadly agree on who were the most prominent and influential calligraphers before big changes began to take place in the art during the 1980s. As in Western art, however, there is less of a consensus about which artists might best represent the last two decades of the twentieth century. Quite often, the choice is based on personal preferences of style. Moreover, one should always remember that China is a huge country; often calligraphers in Beijing know little or nothing about those who are practising in Shanghai, and vice versa.

The task of deciding which contemporary calligraphers to include in this book was not an easy one. I should like to emphasize, therefore, that the contemporary artists included were chosen specifically to illustrate the main trends in calligraphy. The selection does not constitute an exhaustive list of China's current leading calligraphers.

Although much has been written on calligraphy and calligraphers in modern China, it is often difficult to obtain a good overall understanding of an artist and his work from this material. The bulk of this book is based on personal interviews that I have conducted in China over the past eight years. I talked at length with all the contemporary calligraphers about their lives and their art. In the case of those who are dead, I interviewed relatives, friends, former students or Chinese scholars who had studied their work.

During these interviews I spent much of my time trying to establish what the artist wished to convey in a particular piece. This is an important issue, as Chinese poetry, especially classical poetry, is often rich in ambiguity and so can be read in different ways. In such cases, the first reading I have used is that given to me by the artist. Another difficulty in translation stems from the wide-ranging and complex allusions used in the Chinese classics. To avoid lengthy commentaries when faced with this issue, I have worked with leading translators to highlight the sense of such pieces without doing

These details illustrate the extent of variation between the principal trends in Chinese calligraphy. The variations are even more apparent when the four works are compared.

1 Classical, by Wang Shixiang (detail of fig. 97, pp. 158–9)

2 Modernist, by Gu Gan
(detail of fig. 25, p. 31)

3 Neo-Classical, by Han Yu
(detail of fig. 120, pp. 212–3)

4 Avant-Garde, by Wei Ligang
(detail of fig. 142, p. 248)

violence to the original text. Sometimes this has involved inserting some words of explanation into the translation. I hope that these translations will enhance the pleasure of readers when looking at the illustrations. For those who wish to read the original texts, they are given in printed form at the end of this book.

In the period covered by this book, much fine calligraphy has been produced – and is still being produced – by Chinese artists living in Taiwan, Hong Kong, Singapore and the United States. The work of some of these artists has been highly innovative, and highly influential on the mainland; calligraphy from Taiwan was influential even before 1949. However, the work produced beyond the mainland was done in very different circumstances. I felt, therefore, that it would be inappropriate to try to encompass that most interesting aspect of the subject in this book.

Many of my Chinese friends are justly proud of how much they know about Western art. Equally, they are regularly disappointed by how little so many Westerners know about Chinese painting and calligraphy. I hope that by helping readers to experience the pleasures of calligraphy in modern China this book will begin to redress the balance.

1 THE GREAT DEBATE

Over the past fifty years there have been greater changes in the art of calligraphy than in the previous thousand years. Its consequent transformation represents one of the most dynamic developments in the whole history of Chinese art. Because calligraphy is so ancient and revered, much debate has been aroused; the arguments over its definition and purpose will probably rage for decades to come.

Within this debate there are four fairly distinct points of view, broadly representing the main styles of calligraphy practised in China today – the Classical, Modernist, Neo-Classical and Avant-Garde (for examples of these styles, see pp. 12–13). Although these precise terms are not widely used in China, they are helpful tools in trying to understand the issues and appreciate the different voices involved in the debate.

Classical calligraphers, as the term suggests, wish to preserve as many of the old values as possible, while the Neo-Classicists seek to revive and refresh the ancient tradition. At the other end of the spectrum, the Modernists explore radical approaches to the structure and content of the art, and the Avant-Garde, as in other countries, seek to open up new forms of expression and overthrow conventional thinking.

Although these styles are distinct, they are not mutually exclusive. Not only do they all coexist in China today, but many artists delight in crossing boundaries and working in two or more styles. The appellations Classicist and Neo-Classicist therefore need to be used with particular care, since at times it is debatable whether a particular piece should be classed as highly innovative Classical calligraphy or as a Neo-Classical creation.

Beneath these differences there remains a broad consensus about the art of calligraphy itself. In the Chinese mind and the Chinese eye there is a close link between music, dance, Chinese opera and calligraphy. Some talk about calligraphy as an art in which 'the brush dances and the ink sings', others refer to it as a form of 'music without sound'. All agree that it is a performance art in which the ink leaves tangible traces of feeling and expression on the paper. By appreciating the ideas conveyed by these evocative descriptions, Westerners can more easily understand some of the pleasure the Chinese derive from calligraphy – both in the making of it and in the viewing of it.

The Chinese have a special advantage in appreciating calligraphy. Most people who enjoy music cannot play it; nor can all those who like painting paint. But almost all Chinese interested in calligraphy will have at least a practical knowledge of how the art is created, for they will employ the same characters in their own writing.

Even if a Chinese person only knows how to write characters with a pen, he or she will have learned the strict order in which the strokes of each character must be written and so understands the structure lying at the heart of the art form. As a result, most Chinese can share in the excitement of a piece because they understand how it has been put together. Even as they look at a piece of calligraphy, those who themselves know how to use a brush have the added pleasure of being able to sense in their fingers the changing speed and pressure with which the artist moved the brush as he worked his way over the paper.

In some respects, however, the Chinese know too much. When they look at a piece of calligraphy they are immediately struck by its meaning. This is sometimes a disadvantage, for it distracts the eye from the sheer artistry of the composition and the brushwork

The current debate, which started in the mid-1980s, needs to be seen against the background of the history of calligraphy, which stretches back over 3,500 years. The views expressed by the protagonists, however, are not only about art, but also about a wide range of other issues, including the legacy of Chinese history and society, the extent to which Chinese culture should be cross-fertilized with that of other countries and how people should express their feelings.

Setting the scene

Although we now speak of calligraphy as an art form, it was not always considered in this light. The pictograms from which calligraphy first evolved around 1400 BC were created to record and communicate ideas. Initially, calligraphy was a script used for divination, a role linked to the myth that written characters had been a gift from Heaven to humans, but one that could be understood only by those who were divinely inspired, that is, the shamans and the rulers who employed them.

In later centuries calligraphy was used more widely as one element in the exercise of centralized political power through large and well-ordered bureaucracies. All members of the ruling class were expected to be able not only to read characters, but also to write them well. As early as the Tang dynasty (618–906), calligraphy became a key element in the examinations for entry into the Chinese imperial civil service, and it remained so until the end of the nineteenth century. In this way, calligraphy became one of the attributes of the ruling elite.

The art of writing well has been treated with greater reverence for longer in China than in any other civilization. One major reason for this is that in China the power of the written word was not challenged by a culture of political oratory, as it was in the West. Never in China's long history has there been an equivalent of the Areopagus, where the great Athenian political debates took place, or of the Roman Senate. Nor has there been a political orator such as Demosthenes or Cicero. Chinese rulers expressed their power and promulgated their views through written edicts.

As the Chinese developed their written language, they did not switch to using an alphabet; instead, they continued to use characters. The Chinese language quickly acquired tens of thousands of these characters, in which the number of strokes ranged from one to more than twenty-eight. A great deal of thought had to be given to how each individual character could be written easily and legibly, while remaining in harmony with the overall style of a particular document.

Calligraphy first came to be recognized as an art in China during the first century AD and established itself as such between the third and the sixth centuries. During this period the lands to the south of the Yangzi River were ruled by a series of short-lived Chinese kingdoms. The relative weakness of their 'kings' enabled the social elite in southern China to enjoy more freedom. The brushes and papers that were already available provided them with an easy means by which to record their feelings, while the scripts that were then in use enabled them to convert these feelings into a visual art.

Calligraphy was ranked alongside poetry as one of the highest forms of art. Since the eighth century there has been debate over the aesthetics of calligraphy, livelier than that over painting. For painting the point of reference was always nature, whereas for calligraphy it was inevitably more metaphysical because calligraphy is an abstract form of art. The debate ranged over the use of line, ink, composition, the spirit of the work and the influence of the personality of the writer on the calligraphy itself. In the process, new ideas about aesthetics were developed.

The four scripts that were in use by the fourth century AD offered a wide range of artistic possibilities. Regular script (*kai shu*) is upright, with a simple clarity and elegance. Clerical script (*li shu*) has a balance and a gravitas that make it suitable for weighty pronouncements. Running script (*xing shu*) is executed with just sufficient speed to make it possible for the writer to 'run' the strokes together and so create a flow of line and a variety of form that excite the eye. Cursive script (*cao shu*), which was

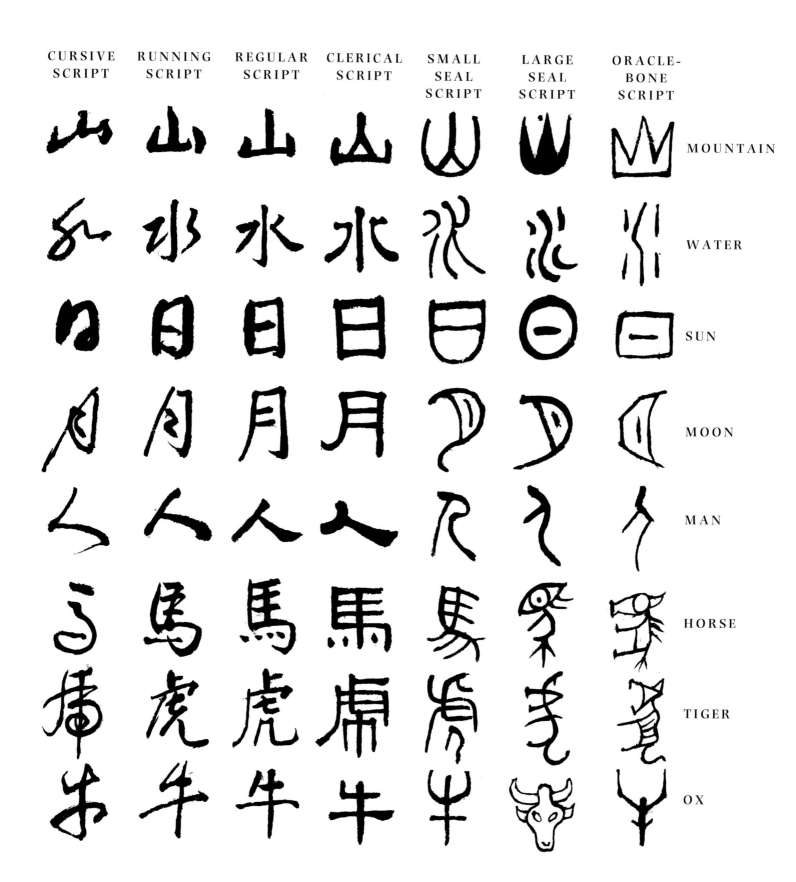

CURSIVE SCRIPT	RUNNING SCRIPT	REGULAR SCRIPT	CLERICAL SCRIPT	SMALL SEAL SCRIPT	LARGE SEAL SCRIPT	ORACLE-BONE SCRIPT	
山	山	山	山	山	山	山	MOUNTAIN
水	水	水	水	水	水	水	WATER
日	日	日	日	日	日	日	SUN
月	月	月	月	月	月	月	MOON
人	人	人	人	人	人	人	MAN
馬	馬	馬	馬	馬	馬	馬	HORSE
虎	虎	虎	虎	虎	虎	虎	TIGER
牛	牛	牛	牛	牛	牛	牛	OX

5 This illustration by Huang Miaozi shows eight different characters written in seven of the eight scripts referred to on the opposite page. The style that is not illustrated is bronze script, which is often quite similar to oracle-bone script.

A BRIEF HISTORY OF CHINESE CALLIGRAPHY

The earliest known form of Chinese writing, called oracle-bone script (*jiaguwen*), dates from the thirteenth to the eleventh century BC. These terse ancient texts, which primarily record acts of divination performed on behalf of the ruler, were incised on tortoise shells and the flat bones of certain animals. Because the bones were discovered and deciphered by archaeologists in the early part of the twentieth century, this ancient script has only recently rejoined the calligraphic tradition.

Bronze script (*jinwen*) appears on bronze vessels and metal weapons and implements dating from the eleventh to the third centuries BC. Having numerous regional variants and styles, bronze script is the earliest form of writing in which a substantial number and variety of texts survive. Cast or inlaid in metal, writing during this phase of development was increasingly used as an important decorative element.

Seal script (*zhuan shu*), so named because it was the style of script used on ancient identity seals, exists in two major forms. The earlier form, known as large seal script, is found on stone inscriptions dating from around the fifth to the third century BC. The later and more common form, called small seal script, was specifically devised under the First Emperor of Qin (reigned 221–210 BC) to create a standardized system of writing. Small seal script is the earliest type in which a large number of handwritten texts, mainly government documents on wood and bamboo, have survived.

Clerical script (*li shu*) also evolved towards the end of the first millennium BC and remained in common use throughout the Han dynasty (206 BC–AD 220). As the name implies, this form of writing was generally used in the preparation of offical records and documents, but it also served as a vehicle for both private correspondence and inscriptions on public monuments. Clerical script was actually a simplifed variation of seal script, in which elements derived from the use of brush and ink, such as hooked and tapered strokes, became considerably more prominent.

Regular script (*kai shu*), which in turn developed from clerical, was first practised in the immediate post-Han period. Combining distinct individual strokes to form symmetrically balanced and clearly legible characters, it has the most sophisticated and complicated forms of any commonly used handwritten Chinese script. Regular script was perfected during the mid-Tang dynasty (618–906) and is still in common use. The first script taught to schoolchildren, it serves as the typeface for most modern printed material.

Running, or semi-cursive, script (*xing shu*), which also appeared in the immediate post-Han period, reached the final stage of its formidable development in the fourth century AD. In running script, many individual strokes are eliminated or condensed, and separate characters may be joined by so-called linking strokes. Because of its convenience, running script quickly became the most popular form of Chinese handwriting in everyday use, which it remains to the present.

Cursive script (*cao shu*) began to develop in the late Han and immediate post-Han period. Although the basic elements of the cursive script were in place by the fourth century, important innovations continued until the mid-Tang dynasty. In cursive script the individual brushstrokes within a character are dramatically abbreviated, often becoming a single continuous impulse of the writer's brush. Because the number and order of strokes are significantly altered, the writing and reading of cursive script have always required special training.

Shen C. Y. Fu
FORMER SENIOR CURATOR OF CHINESE ART, FREER GALLERY OF ART, WASHINGTON, D.C.

originally a draft script, represents a speedy, powerful and more dramatic form of art.

By this time, for well over a thousand years calligraphy had been written from top to bottom and from right to left, with the characters neatly lined up both vertically and horizontally. These conventions date from the eighth to the sixth centuries BC, when characters were written with a brush on strips of bamboo held in the left hand. After each one was completed, it was placed to the right of the writer so that he could see clearly what he had just written while he continued to write.

In the centuries that elapsed between the end of the Han dynasty in 220 and the beginning of the Qing dynasty in 1644, many fine pieces of calligraphy were produced in China by artists, monks, scholar-officials, and occasionally by emperors. A small number of people were particularly influential. The list of who they were is open to debate, but short lists rarely exclude those names mentioned below.

First and foremost is Wang Xizhi (303–361), who is widely regarded as China's most distinguished calligrapher. He was highly innovative and went beyond the stage of putting his personal imprint on a style of calligraphy; he consciously sought to create something different that was unquestionably a work of art. His new style of running script is extraordinarily beautiful (fig. 6). It is renowned for the light fluidity of the brushwork and the exquisite balance that he achieved, both in the way the strokes were arranged within a character and in the overall composition of the piece. In addition, his work was full of variety. If he used the same character more than once within a piece, he would change the form while remaining within the overall style he was using.

In the Tang dynasty there were two markedly different trends: one towards discipline and order and the other towards spontaneity and exuberance. The former was exemplified by General Yan Zhenqing (709–785), who made his own rather vigorous and powerful interpretation of the regular script created a century or so earlier, which eventually became the principal model from which all later generations learned to write (fig. 7). His script was clear, masculine and bold, and his rounded strokes easier and quicker to write than the straight ones used in clerical script. General Yan played a key part in promoting the idea that good calligraphy could only be written by people who held their brush properly, and only people of moral rectitude, he said, could do that. In other words, calligraphy would be a mirror of the moral quality of the person who wrote it.

At about the same time that General Yan was establishing his enduring style of regular script, Zhang Xu (active 710–750) and the 'mad monk'

6 Wang Xizhi's running script.

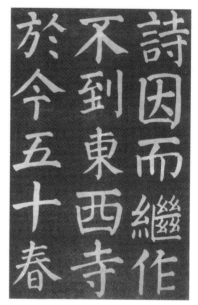

7 Yan Zhenqing's regular script.

8 Huaisu's wild cursive script.

9 Mi Fu's vibrant three-dimensional cursive script.

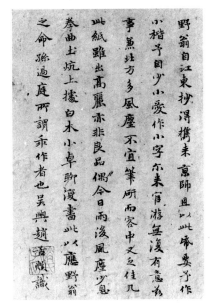

10 Zhao Mengfu's regular script.

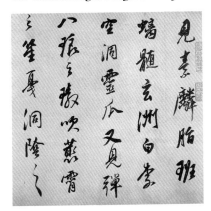

11 Dong Qichang's painterly use of inks in running script.

Huaisu (725–785) were creating a new and dramatic form of calligraphy, 'wild cursive script'. Zhang Xu was renowned for his alcoholically inspired performances of calligraphy, done at great speed; they were charged with strong emotion and rhythm, with dramatic changes between characters written in thick and thin strokes. Huaisu's calligraphy was also notable for its speed of execution, emotion and rhythm, but his strokes were thinner and lighter, often with long vertical strokes plunging down the paper before he began the next character (fig. 8).

In the Song dynasty (960–1279) another eccentric calligrapher rose to prominence. Mi Fu (1051–1107) was so skilled at replicating the styles of the masters of the past that the emperor honoured him with a position at court. Although Mi Fu could easily copy the tightly regulated clerical and regular scripts of earlier calligraphers, his own work was vibrant. It reflected his belief that the writing of calligraphy should be as spontaneous and lively as the experience of riding a horse without a bridle or saddle. Not only did he vary the size of his characters, he also combined heavy strokes with light and often succeeded in making his characters appear three-dimensional (fig. 9). He was a master of calculated risk.

In 1286, seven years after the collapse of the Song dynasty, Zhao Mengfu (1254–1322), a descendant of one of the Song emperors, agreed to serve as a minister in the Yuan dynasty (1279–1368) that had been established by the victorious Mongols. In calligraphy he synthesized past traditions into a new form of regular script. Unlike the rather stiff styles of the Tang dynasty, Zhao's had an airy brightness, which reflected the warm smoothness that had characterized much of Song art. His skill in both calligraphy and painting led him to become the first person to use calligraphic techniques in painting (fig. 10).

Three hundred years later, another distinguished calligrapher and painter, Dong Qichang (1555–1636), served briefly, though unsuccessfully, as a minister during the Ming dynasty (1368–1644). Dong devoted much time to studying the works of past masters. However, instead of copying the exact structure of individual characters and the overall composition of a work, he created new forms of calligraphy by interpreting their spirit. Whereas Zhao Mengfu had introduced calligraphic technique into painting, Dong did the reverse. He was the first to introduce into calligraphy the wide range of ink effects used by painters. He particularly liked to work with a thin ink to create slim and elegant characters, which he linked together with dynamic energy (fig. 11).

Even after the fall of the Ming dynasty, the mastery of calligraphy still involved studying closely the achievements of its most revered practitioners, the majority of whom had lived before the tenth century AD. This grounding of contemporary art in the past not only illustrates the profound respect the Chinese have for the pioneers of this ancient art, but also shows the deeply conservative nature of the society in which it developed (fig. 12). It has to be said, however, that the characters of the Chinese script are man-made, so, unlike the objects in a painting, they necessarily remain the only models for the aspiring calligrapher to follow.

Despite the weight of conservative tradition, calligraphy as an art form reached a new peak of achievement in the latter part of the Qing dynasty (1644–1911), which had been established by the Manchus. One of the means by which China's new rulers sought to reinforce their legitimacy was by promoting the study of China's calligraphic heritage. This encouraged several leading Chinese scholars to take a greater interest in this field, which appealed to their sense of cultural superiority while not bringing them into conflict with their despotic rulers.

New studies of ancient inscriptions on bronze and stone, popular in the early Qing dynasty, led to some lively innovations in script. So, too, did the late nineteenth-century discovery of large numbers of oracle bones bearing thousands of ancient pictograms that had not previously been known. At the same time, a number of leading Chinese calligraphers, particularly Kang Youwei (1858–1927), gradually moved away from the strong epigraphic style towards a greater freedom of expression. This forceful and free style laid the foundation for the revival of cursive script in the twentieth century.

The innovations that had begun in the latter part of the Qing dynasty continued into Republican China (1912–49). Li Shutong (1880–1942), who in his late thirties became a Buddhist monk, blended regular and running scripts into a new, gentle, naive style that conveyed some of the inner calm of his Buddhist beliefs. The painter Wu Changshuo (1844–1927), on the other hand, created wonderfully refreshing and powerful pieces that were inspired by his study of the ancient bronze and seal scripts. Qi Baishi (1863–1957), another renowned painter, drew inspiration from ancient characters, which he then worked into forms that were almost abstract paintings. He also created exquisite compositions in which he combined painting with innovative calligrapy. The text was often riotously funny or bitingly sharp.

The most reform-minded calligrapher of the early twentieth century was Yu Youren (1879–1964), who believed that the Nationalist Party led by Jiang Jieshi (Chiang Kaishek) could reform and modernize China. The Party's slogan for the development of China was 'New, Fast, Strong,

22

12 For centuries Chinese children have learnt calligraphy by writing characters within boxes, in order to understand their structure and proportions.

Simple'. Yu argued that in order for this policy to succeed, China needed to modify its calligraphy so that it could be learnt more easily and written more quickly.

Yu proposed that this should be done by standardizing cursive script, a task he completed in the late 1930s after many years of research. His imaginative idea was not adopted by the Nationalists, who by that time were preoccupied with their struggle against both the Communists and the Japanese. However, the simplified characters introduced by the new Chinese Communist government in 1956 drew on his ideas.

These innovations failed to change the deeply conservative outlook of most calligraphers. Although the 'May Fourth Movement' of 1919 succeeded in opening up more Chinese arts to Western ideas and styles, even innovative calligraphers continued to regard calligraphy as a wholly indigenous art form, for which exposure to outside influences held no benefits. This general attitude persisted until the creation of New China in 1949, and indeed for many years after that.

For centuries, calligraphy displayed within a home or more publicly had been deemed an acceptable vehicle for the expression of Confucian values, Buddhist beliefs and Daoist philosophy. It was also a popular medium for elegiac poetry, because such verse provided pleasure for those who were in power and solace for those who were not. In general, it was socially unacceptable to voice deep personal feelings in calligraphy displayed where other people could see it. Nevertheless, Chinese Chan (Zen) Buddhists wrote about their intense emotional experience in achieving 'enlightenment', and in the late Ming dynasty personal feelings were more openly expressed in calligraphy.

Under the tight censorship which prevailed during the Qing dynasty it was politically dangerous to voice dissent. Those who wished to express such feelings resorted to the innuendo and subtle allusions that could be achieved by reworking words from classical poetry, history and literature. In Republican China some calligraphers did begin to express their feelings more explicitly in their works, but the main vehicle of expression had now become cartoons and prose written in the style of the spoken language, not the traditional classical one.

Creating calligraphy

The 'four treasures' of a Chinese scholar's studio have long been paper, brushes, inksticks and inkstones (fig. 13). Although there are similar implements in the West, the effects that can be produced with the Chinese versions are very different.

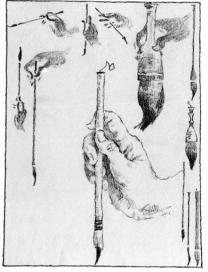

13 The 'four treasures' of the scholar's studio: paper, brush, inkstick and inkstone.

14 An illustration of some of the wide variety of brushes used by Chinese calligraphers.

Chinese calligraphy paper is known as *xuan* paper. The subtle structure of this material allows water to spread rapidly across its surface, while at the same time slowing the movement of the particles suspended in the ink. Although paper was invented in the Western Han period (221–206 BC), large sheets of it were not made until the Ming dynasty.

Calligraphy is usually written on plain white *xuan* paper. Glossier papers decorated with suitably spaced roundels or medallions are quite often used as a setting for the characters in a couplet. Silk is the most luxurious background, but although characters written on it in a rich, black ink look most elegant, silk (which is much less absorbent than paper) does not lend itself well to the use of more varied ink effects.

Chinese brushes range in size from those with a tip as fine as a needle to those as tall as a man that produce brushstrokes more than a metre wide (fig. 14). The different types of hair used in calligraphy brushes also allow a wide range of effects, some being especially well suited to particular types of script. The main difference between the brushwork of Chinese calligraphers and that of Western painters is that the former use the tip of the brush to create a line – which is the essence of calligraphy – whereas the latter tend to use the side of a flatter brush to build up layers of paint.

Chinese inksticks are made of soot mixed with resin. The ink is produced by grinding the stick on the wet surface of an inkstone. The resulting substance has three notable properties: it does not fade, once it is dry it will not run even when in contact with water, and it can produce an extraordinary range of effects when used on Chinese *xuan* paper.

The inkstones are usually carved out of black stone with a surface just rough enough to enable the artist to grind the ink into small particles, which, if required, can be made finer by further grinding. Inkstones are considered treasures, not only because of the important part they play in the process of calligraphy, but also because they are often elegantly carved to bring out the natural markings of the stone.

Traditional calligraphers rely on six main effects. 'Dark ink' creates a solid, lustrous black, while 'light ink', as one would expect, produces a paler line. The use of 'dry ink' results in the hairs of the brush soon separating to leave white streaks within the brushstroke, while 'wet ink' creates a softer-edged line. With 'overnight ink', on the other hand, the heavier and lighter particles become separated and can therefore produce a brushstroke with a dark inner core or 'bone', which is surrounded by a soft 'flesh'. 'Parched ink', which is both dark and dry, creates a strong line that is streaked with white (fig. 15).

Informally, there is a fifth 'treasure' – and that is the seal. The Chinese have transformed the use of personal seals into an art form that adorns both calligraphy and painting. Not only do they devote much artistry to carving their seals, but the red ink that is used to transfer these impressions on to the paper makes a beautiful coloured counterpoint to texts traditionally rendered in black ink on white paper. Often calligraphers will use several seals on a single work. One will probably bear the artist's family and personal name (*xingming*), another may show his formal name (*zi*), usually given to him on reaching adulthood by an older relative or friend, while a third could carry a 'nickname' (*hao*) describing the particular traits or interests of the artist.

The Classicists

The admirers of classical calligraphy in modern China regard it as an art of exquisite refinement and the ultimate expression of Chinese culture. They delight in its antiquarian flavour and erudite forms of expression, and admire most those practitioners who excel in combining an excellence of technique with a mastery of poetry.

The Classicists believe that the styles of calligraphy developed in the past provide a rich variety of themes on which the talented can perform endless variations. Traditionally, these variations did not involve mixing styles; instead, the variations were intended to reflect the personality of the artist working within a recognized style (see figs 16 and 17).

Over the centuries the Chinese have both chronicled and analysed the long history and complex evolution of classical calligraphy. There are literally thousands of books covering every aspect of the subject. These topics merit more space than they can be allocated in a book about the

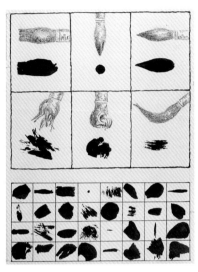

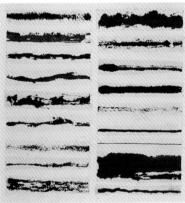

15 Chinese brushes enable calligraphers to create a much greater variety of lines and dots than is possible with a Western brush.

16 This piece of classical-style calligraphy by Wang Shixiang (explained on p. 157) illustrates the traditional format, with the vertical columns of characters running from right to left.

17 Here, Shen Yinmo is shown instructing Liu Zengfu in the finer points of brush technique, in 1962.

art of calligraphy in modern China, but for those who are interested I have included in the bibliography some of the excellent English-language books on this subject.

The Classicists generally use thick black ink, which they can work into the paper to make their characters stand out clearly. But a skilled calligrapher can use such ink to create a whole range of moods. Shen Yinmo, for example, could write characters which the famous calligrapher Sun Guoting (648?–703?) would have praised for being so sharp that you felt chilled when you looked at them (fig. 18), or so soft that they brought to mind the blush on a young girl's cheek or a pearl of dew on a lotus leaf (fig. 19).

Amongst the Classical calligraphers in modern China, Qi Gong (pp. 146–52) has been admired for his innovative approach to the shaping of his characters. He made them more pert by writing them according to new

18, 19 The brushwork of Shen Yinmo could be either sharp and chilling (top) or soft and blushing.

ratios of proportions that emphasized their verticality (fig. 20). He also used a mixture of thick and thin strokes to create tensions that generate an unusual excitement in his running script. Huang Miaozi (pp. 172–81), on the other hand, often takes one of the ancient forms of script that were originally carved or etched and then rewrites them with a brush in, say, running script, which gives them an unexpected liveliness.

Calligraphers are not just concerned with the individual characters, however; they are also interested in the patterns those characters create on the paper. Some calligraphers delight in the regular pattern created by uniform, evenly-spaced characters. Westerners generally like this style, but the Chinese have seen a surfeit of such calligraphy and will usually save their praise for those pieces that contain 'something extra'. This is most often the tension and energy generated by asymmetrical compositions, which reflect the artist's vitality and experience of life.

The overall composition of a piece is often discussed in musical terms. Viewers look to see whether the different elements have been successfully integrated into a kind of visual symphony through the interplay of black and white spaces and the changing tonalities of the ink. For instance, when the eighty-five-year-old Huang Miaozi saw the work illustrated in fig. 21 (pp. 28–9), after more than a decade, he raised his hands above his head and began to dance a little jig, exclaiming as he did so: 'Wonderful, wonderful, just like a symphony!' On the other hand, when Liu Zengfu (pp. 203–9) looked at a scroll by Sha Menghai (pp. 133–8), he dismissed it with the words: 'There's no music in it – it's doh, doh, doh, all the way through.'

Content was a difficult issue for Classical calligraphers in China after the Communist takeover of 1949. In the first three decades of New China, calligraphers had little scope for free expression. Some happily provided words to support the new regime, while others stuck to copying out innocuous classical poems. The poetry of Mao Zedong (pp. 105–17) genuinely appealed to many calligraphers, who wrote it out endlessly, safe in the knowledge that it was acceptable. A few – for example, Deng Sanmu (pp. 100–104) – did subtly express their own feelings.

In the 1980s and 1990s there was a real renaissance in the content of Classical calligraphy. For example, the poems written by Qi Gong, Huang Miaozi and Wang Shixiang (pp. 153–61) were still classical in flavour, but their content had become more personal, and at times savagely satirical. These three and others wrote about their experiences during the decade of the so-called Cultural Revolution (1966–76), their life since then and religion, as well as recording their reflections on modern society and the pleasures of friendship and nature.

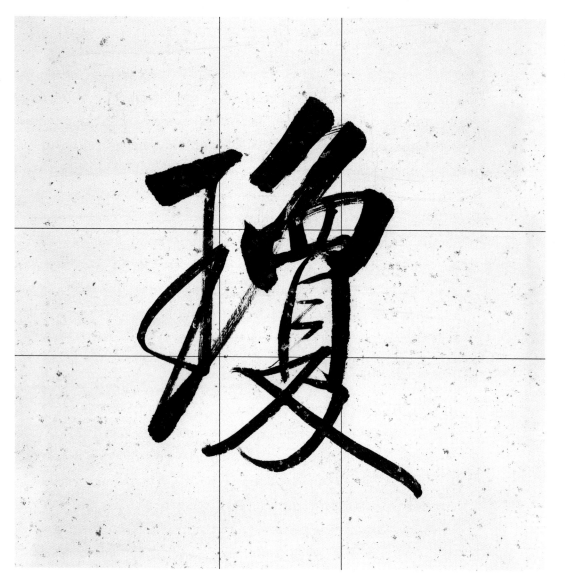

20 The use of the more vertical grid developed by Qi Gong can give characters a livelier appearance.

21 This 180-character scroll by Zhang Zhengyu can be interpreted as a visual musical symphony.

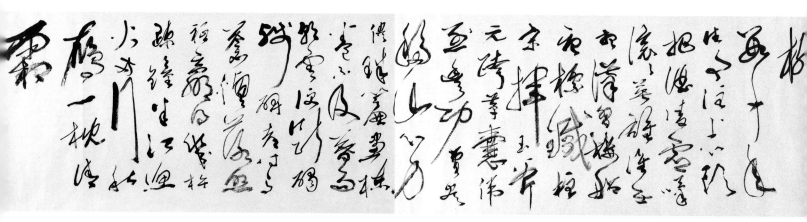

The Modernists

The Modernist movement emerged in the mid-1980s, a time of rapid change and excitement in China. It was driven by frustration and anger about the past, especially the suffering that so many people had endured during the decade of the Cultural Revolution, and encouraged by the new ideas that were flooding into China from the West as a result of Deng Xiaoping's reforms.

The exponents of Modernism believed that calligraphy would never become a means of creative expression in modern China unless it broke free from the rigorous rules that had constrained it for centuries. Modernist calligraphy, they argued, should unashamedly proclaim itself a form of fine art. They intended, therefore, to be more painterly in their whole approach to calligraphy, including the way they structured their characters, the compositions they created and their use of inks (see fig. 22). Instead of being inward-looking, like the calligraphers of the past, they wanted to draw inspiration from other arts, both Chinese and Western.

Although the movement itself only emerged in the mid-1980s, it grew out of the work of five pioneers who had been exploring new possibilities since the mid-1960s. Four of them had started out as painters and the fifth had been a theatrical designer. They, in turn, had drawn inspiration from the experiments of other calligraphers in the first half of the century.

The first was Lu Weizhao (1899–1980), a highly innovative artist who managed to get calligraphy established at the Hangzhou Academy of Fine Art as a subject worthy of scholarly study, not merely one taught as a practical art. The second was Zhang Ding (b. 1917), the only artist from the People's Republic of China to have met Picasso (see pp. 53–4). The third was Zhang Zhengyu (pp. 119–24), who brought his theatrical eye to the design of characters and the spatial relationships between them. The fourth was Li Luogong (pp. 125–31), who had studied Western avant-garde

art, and the last was Shi Lu (1919–82) who, as he declined through alcoholism into madness, made his characters seem as if they were exploding.

The Modernists pointed out that Chinese characters, which had been written in many different ways by various artists over the centuries, could be made even more interesting artistically. Gu Gan (pp. 182–93) demonstrated this by presenting forty-six alternative versions of the character for 'mountain' (*shan*) – some of them forms created by famous calligraphers of the past, others his own inventions (fig. 23).

The more complex characters offer even greater scope for conversion to new forms. For example, the proportions of a character can be modified to create a new dynamic in the relationship of the spaces within it or of those between it and other characters. The standard compact form of the character for 'cloud' (*yun*) can be stretched vertically or horizontally (fig. 24). Alternatively, one might exaggerate one part of a character; in the character for 'orchid' (*lan*), for instance, the upper part usually quietly takes up a third of the space occupied by the whole. Here (fig. 25) it has been enlarged to fill two-thirds of the space dramatically, albeit with the help of innovative ink techniques.

Wherever possible, therefore, Modernists like to reshape characters in order to reinforce their meaning. This has been done not only with clouds

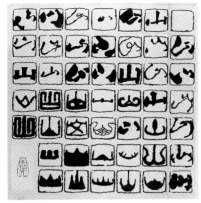

23 Forty-six ways in which the Chinese character for the word 'mountain' (*shan*) can be written.

24, 25 The Modernists like to reshape characters in new ways – 'cloud' (left), 'orchid' (right).

and orchids, but also with other subjects from nature, such as tigers (see fig. 99, p. 167). This reshaping is often done by linking back to the earliest forms of writing, based on pictograms.

Another approach is to use the old Daoist technique of blending two well-known characters together to form a new one. Figures 26 and 27 show how Sa Benjie (pp. 216–25) has done this with the characters *jue* ('to awake' one's senses through the eye) and *wu* ('to awake' one's senses through the heart), which together mean 'realization' or 'enlightenment' in Chinese. Because Sa believes that true realization stems from the use of both senses, he likes the idea of writing them as a single character.

Instead of using the conventional thick black ink with its lustrous sheen, so loved by the Classicists, the Modernists seek to exploit the full range of effects that have long been known to Chinese painters, including the use of coloured inks. The range of possibilities is enormous. For example, a line simply written in solid black becomes much more interesting when flecked with water (fig. 28); striking effects can be achieved by using dark ink across lighter ink that is still wet (fig. 29); and by using a brush so loaded with watery ink that the water oozes into the paper beyond the ink, it is possible to impede the flow of ink from a second brushstroke, thereby creating a whitish halo effect (fig. 30).

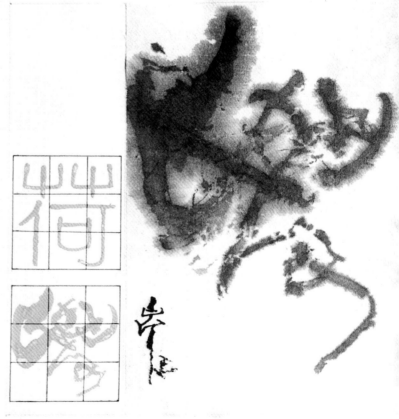

In line with their painterly approach, Modernists tend to use relatively few characters. Their works will often, however, carry layers of meaning – ranging from ones that conjure up beautifully soothing images to religious or philosophical ideas, or expressions of the artist's attitudes on various issues. In these compositions the characters are not meant to be an explanation in prose of an idea or a sentiment, but are used as symbols that are intended to open up ideas in the mind of the viewer about what it is that he or she is seeing.

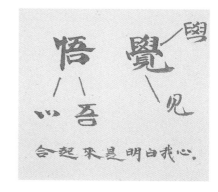

26, 27 Sa Benjie attempts to make people think by joining two characters together into one. In the first illustration above, the two characters *jue* and *wu* are seen separately; in the second, they have been combined.

Gu Gan's 1991 piece *World of Supreme Bliss* (fig. 22) conveys the message in the title in several different ways. The large image of Buddha, rendered in red with a seal, induces an air of calm. So, too, do the characters written across the work – *Ji Le Shi Jie* – which mean 'World of Supreme Bliss', a well-known Buddhist phrase that refers to the state of mind achieved by rejecting the material world and seeking inner peace. The images on the seals that Gu Gan carved specially for this composition are a reminder of the glorious Buddhist works of art created in China. Many of these can be seen at Dunhuang, the famous monastery situated on the Silk Road, along which Buddhism first entered the country.

The Modernists hope not only that China will absorb more of the culture of other countries, but that Chinese culture will increasingly be appreciated internationally. Naturally, they want calligraphy to be part of this ideal and to act as a bridge in achieving it. The fact that some of the works by

28, 29, 30 China's Modernist calligraphers create a fascinating variety of ink effects.

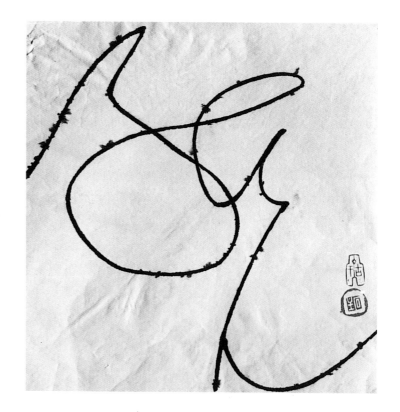

Miró and other Western abstract painters look almost like modern Chinese calligraphy encourages this aspiration. So, too, does the importance of line in much recent Western abstract art.

The Neo-Classicists

In Europe the architects of the Renaissance period were inspired by Roman remains that were a thousand years old or more. Equally, the neo-classical architects of the eighteenth and early nineteenth centuries wanted to revive the even older and purer styles of ancient Greece. Neo-Classical calligraphy in China emerged in very different circumstances.

At the end of the twentieth century there still remained a handful of elderly Classical calligraphers in China. Even so, there was no possibility of maintaining the Grand Tradition they represented. The whole society and culture that had sustained the art of calligraphy for almost 2,000 years had all but vanished within the past half-century. Although politics played its part in the demise of Classical calligraphy (as is explained in the next chapter), the main cause was modernization.

In the modern age it was inconceivable that the Chinese would continue to write with a brush, let alone spend hours every day practising using one. There was no longer time for people to learn the classics by heart, or encouragement for them to write their own poetry. As in Western countries, there was a general decline in the ability to analyse one's feelings

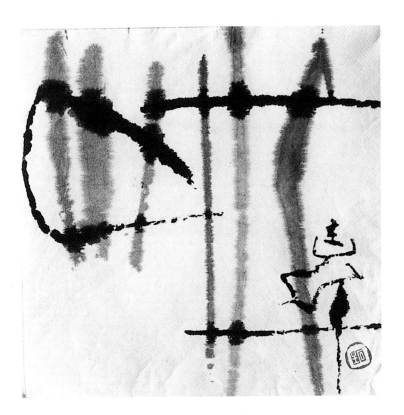

and express them with refinement and elegance – and without these capabilities, artists could not hope to match the most admired social graces of traditional Chinese society. They would simply not develop the mental agility that would enable them to combine phrases from different works into beautifully matched couplets or to rework them elegantly to suit some new situation.

The ending of the classical tradition did, however, open up exciting opportunities to refresh an ancient art and make it accessible to a modern audience still enthralled by the richness of Chinese culture. The Neo-Classicists took to heart the words of the famous painter Shi Tao (1642–1710), who said that 'the ink should follow the times'.

Few Neo-Classical calligraphers believe that they will ever be able to match the mastery of the brush that was achieved by the great practitioners of the past. Nevertheless, they feel free to push forward experiments with the classical styles of calligraphy, like the innovators of the first half of the twentieth century, by modifying the structure of the characters, using a wider range of ink effects, taking a more painterly approach to composition and choosing their words with care.

Zhang Sen (pp. 195–202) elongates his clerical script characters horizontally (fig. 31). Another approach involves not only modifying the shape of the characters, but also being more painterly in the use of ink. Instead of using solid black ink, for instance, Han Yu (pp. 210–15) brings his characters to life by giving them a looser structure and writing them out in inks that are full of subtleties.

The majority of Neo-Classical works pay homage to the Grand Tradition. Sometimes an artist will follow closely the style of one of the great masters of the past, but the more imaginative will use the inspiration they have derived from the past to create something fresh (fig. 32).

Although most Neo-Classical calligraphy is written in the traditional format of vertical columns (and occasionally horizontal panels that are written from left to right), some artists have varied the size of characters and placed them on the paper in different positions to make them look more interesting. In works of this sort the centre of the composition may feature just one, two or three characters, conveying such ideas as gentle rain, fleeting clouds, or some broader concept that is explained by a line of verse written in much smaller script. At this point there is an overlap between the works produced in this style by the Neo-Classicists and those done by the early Modernists.

The attraction of a Neo-Classical piece is often greatly enhanced by the elegance of its content. Zhang Sen, who is one of the leaders in this field,

31 Zhang Sen gives his clerical script a fresh look by stretching out his characters horizontally and making his brushstrokes more dynamic. In this piece the words are by the Tang poet Wang Wei (701–761):

Walk up to the source of the stream and
Then just sit there and watch the clouds
*   gathering above.*

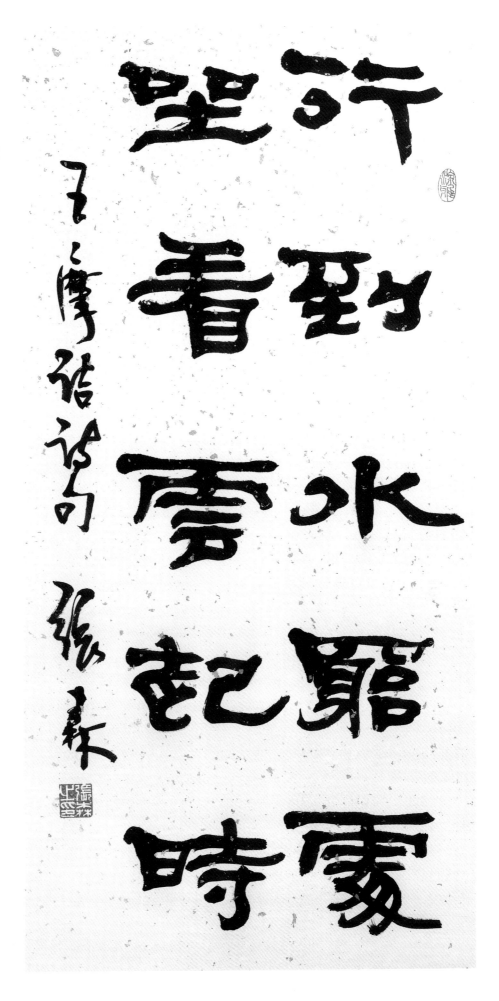

insists that because calligraphy is an art, its content can never be the text of a mundane letter to one's mother or something as banal as a laundry list. There must, as he puts it, 'be magic in the words', and there is no lack of such magic in Chinese poetry.

The Neo-Classicists are particularly fond of the poetry of the Tang and Song dynasties, which expressed a broad range of sentiments – from heart-rending feelings of love or sorrow to sharply worded protests about the various injustices of the time. In modern China there are no constraints on having such poems adorning one's walls, and many of them are widely known. The few calligraphers who are attracted to modern poetry will only use it when writing for themselves or for similarly-minded friends.

The Avant-Garde

The artists of the Avant-Garde have a different agenda from the Modernists. By definition, their aim, like that of the avant-garde in other countries, is to explore new frontiers for their art. Through the use of novel techniques, the creation of adventurous compositions and the expression of contemporary ideas, they want to produce works that command attention in order to make people reflect upon a subject or to challenge conventional thinking. In some works the statements being made are explicit, in others they are implicit. The art of allusion lives on in China, even among the ranks of the Avant-Garde.

To some extent, the challenge they face revolves around the nature of calligraphy itself. Certain members of the Avant-Garde, such as Pu Lieping (pp. 236–43), will occasionally incorporate into their works the earliest Chinese pictograms, which are in a sense symbols (fig. 33). In general, however, the Avant-Garde reject the use of legible characters. Their works are usually accompanied by a title which the artist hopes will evoke the sentiments he experienced as he was creating the brushstrokes.

The more traditionally-minded critics claim that works based on un-readable characters cannot, by definition, be calligraphy, but are instead abstract works of art. Zhang Qiang (pp. 256–63) has responded by arguing that if it is possible for a painting that does not include a representational image to be a painting, then it is equally possible for a work of art that does not have readable characters still to be considered a piece of calligraphy. Furthermore, he points out that the techniques and effects of calligraphy vary in many ways from those of Western abstract art.

Avant-Garde artists reject the use of readable characters for different reasons. In the late 1980s, for example, Xu Bing (b. 1955) began producing huge numbers of printed 'characters' that looked readable, but were

32 In this couplet, written in 1995, Sa Benjie pays homage to the classical calligrapher Yi Bingshou (1754–1815), renowned for the strength of his horizontal lines, the prominence he gave to his dots, and the interplay of spaces between his

characters. Sa Benjie, however, has created his own distinctive style:

Only when you have let yourself sink into complete confusion
Can you start to climb back towards clear-mindedness.

in fact unintelligible, to express his rejection of many aspects of traditional Chinese culture (see p. 57). Qiu Zhenzhong (b. 1947), on the other hand, used a Chinese brush to write nonsensical characters – a device first used by Bai Qianshen in 1981 (see p. 56). Qiu argued that, for the Chinese, readable characters are a distraction from the true magic of calligraphy, which lies in the line of the brush.

Another artist, Wang Nanming (pp. 250–5), has pushed this idea further. He takes sheets of paper on which he has written legible characters and scrunches them up into balls. He then uses the broken lines that can be seen on the outside of each ball to focus attention on the beauty of the brushwork, at the same time creating a whole new form of artistic expression through his use of balls of calligraphy.

The Avant-Garde have been highly inventive in exploring the power and attraction which the calligraphic line holds for the Chinese. Wei Ligang (pp. 244–9; see also fig. 4, p. 13), for instance, knows that when a Chinese viewer looks at something written within the framework of a square, he or she instinctively expects it to be a legible character, because all Chinese children traditionally learned – and many continue to learn – to write out characters in square boxes. Wei exploits this automatic response to focus the viewer's eye not on readable characters, but on artistic forms composed with calligraphic brushwork and ink.

Whereas Wei tends to concentrate on detail in his pieces, the style of Zhang Dawo (pp. 227–35) is more expansive. He has created light, abstract forms that make the ink seem to be flying off the paper. He also makes large, solid forms of black against a white background, which have an unquestionably Chinese feel to them, while at the same time looking to the Western eye like silhouettes of sculptures by Henry Moore.

One artist is well known for taking a more human and intimate approach to the calligraphic line. For Zhang Qiang the trace of the brush on paper represents the movement of one's spirit, but he prefers to let it flow by working together with a young woman. Some of his assistants will move the paper for him while he writes with a brush, others let him use their body as the surface for his art. The result, he claims, is a trace of the creative impulses generated by the interplay between a man and a woman.

Both the Modernists and the Avant-Garde work with a wider range of materials than the traditionalists. They often use new, thick forms of *xuan* paper, which not only has a more interesting surface than the standard sheet, but also allows the creation of a new range of ink effects. Oil and acrylic paints are used by both groups, but only the Avant-Garde have used installations, videos and sculptures (fig. 34).

Within the Avant-Garde movement there are two main types of work: pieces that concentrate on the abstract beauty of calligraphic lines and ink techniques, and those which more explicitly reject the traditional ideas of calligraphy. It may seem strange that artists who love calligraphy seem so set on rejecting the traditions of the past, but they would argue that the art and the tradition are two separate things. For them, calligraphic art is a source of inspiration and beauty, whereas the old cultural tradition of calligraphy equates to some of the darker aspects of Chinese society and culture. These include, above all, being constantly told by your elders what you can and cannot do, pressure to conform, the inward-looking nature of

33 In his abstract work *Pastoral Melodies* (explained on pp. 239–40) Pu Lieping includes early pictograms for 'bird' and 'fish'.

34 As early as 1986, Wu Shanzhuan (b. 1960) brought together in his 'Red Room' a bewildering array of messages that haunted or surprised people in China at that time – political slogans, advertisements, traffic directions, poetry and even weather forecasts.

the subject, rejection of the idea of exploring links with other arts and cultures, and the failure of calligraphy to develop into a vehicle for expression in modern society.

That said, the best-known practitioners of the Avant-Garde – like Picasso and Matisse before them – have a deep knowledge of the classical tradition. Several of them have written extensively on the history of calligraphy and its techniques. Whatever else they are doing, they are not simply splashing paint about.

2 THE CHANGING WORLD

The great changes that have taken place within China over the past fifty years have both reshaped and revitalized calligraphy. At the same time, calligraphy itself has played a surprisingly prominent role in the reshaping of modern China.

New China

In 1949 calligraphy could be seen everywhere (fig. 35). Not only were the streets full of it, many houses were as well. Within a private house there was usually an ancestor altar flanked by calligraphic scrolls and plaques, and the larger reception or living rooms would be decorated with hanging scrolls of calligraphy and paintings. Palaces and temples were bedecked with huge pieces of calligraphy indicating the names of pavilions and gates. There were far more examples of large-scale script to be seen in a Chinese city than there were shop signs and advertising billboards in a Western one. Moreover, nearly all of this script was still handwritten or reproduced by carving.

35 In China the streets were full of shops decorated with carved signs and embroidered banners bearing their names and proclaiming their wares.

The Chinese have always regarded the ability to write good calligraphy as the mark of a well-disciplined, educated and cultivated person. Not only did educated people write with a brush, but they would spend hours every day practising their calligraphy (fig. 36). Such practice served to perfect their style and, by extension, enhance their reputation. It also offered an acceptable form of therapy in a society that provided few outlets for frustration or anger. With the passing of time, pens and pencils were increasingly used for the sake of convenience. But for those who had learnt the sensuous pleasures of the brush, these tools seemed unresponsive instruments.

When Mao Zedong (pp. 105–17) came to power in 1949, both he and several of his colleagues were already widely known as enthusiastic calligraphers. Despite the rigour of the times, most of them managed to amass large collections of fine calligraphy, either as purchases they had made in antique shops (where such pieces could be bought cheaply) or as gifts received from people wishing to curry favour.

Before the Cultural Revolution began in 1966, these Party leaders would often write out for their friends traditional poems covering a wide range of subjects, or they might compose poems of their own, which were usually about the pleasures of nature or visits to famous cultural sites. Occasionally they would write more personal, even humorous, poems for their families.

Within the central bureaucracy the standard of calligraphy was high and writing was nearly always done with a brush. The secretary-general of Mao's Secretariat, Chen Bingchen, was a fine stylist who would not tolerate poor brushwork from his subordinates. The Chinese text of the 'Sino-Soviet Treaty of Peace and Friendship' signed by Mao and Stalin in Moscow in 1950, for example, was not typewritten, but handwritten by Chen with a brush. In these circumstances it is hardly surprising that there was a strong impetus for many of the less well-educated people within the Party to aspire to understand calligraphy and write well.

The interest of China's new leaders in calligraphy might have boded well for the future of the art, had Mao not also been the most revolutionary ruler to which China had ever been subjected. From the outset Mao believed that the culture surrounding calligraphy was synonymous with the elitist and conservative traditions of Old China which he and many of the rank-and-file members of the Party wished to eradicate.

When he came to power, Mao knew that he had won control of a country in which only about fifteen per cent of the population could read anything more than simple texts. This high level of illiteracy was an

36 In the 1950s teachers taught Chinese children to write plain, legible calligraphy with a brush. Many parents gave their children additional tuition at home.

impediment to the modernization of China. The situation was all the more serious because Mandarin Chinese was not widely understood at that time, and local dialects were so different that people were often unable to understand others who lived elsewhere in their own province, let alone further afield. Mao recognized that the written language would have to play a key role in unifying the country.

The need to improve literacy was so great that the leadership even considered abandoning Chinese characters in favour of the Roman alphabet. In the end, Mao decided that Chinese characters had to be retained, as they were such an integral element of the country's culture and history. He was, however, willing to support a compromise whereby the teaching of the spoken language would be facilitated by the adoption of romanization, while the written language would be made easier to write by simplifying those commonly used characters that were composed of many strokes.

The nationalization of private businesses soon changed the look of China's cities and towns. Most of the old colourful calligraphic nameboards and banners were replaced by smaller, less flamboyant ones. Not only was there a slump in the demand for commercial calligraphy, but wealthier people who had previously purchased calligraphy for their own pleasure either fled abroad or were unwilling to buy for fear of political repercussions. Those who had earned their living by producing calligraphy were soon impoverished (see Deng Sanmu, pp. 100–4).

At this stage, these changes did not affect the large number of distinguished scholar-calligraphers. Some were teaching in universities or pursuing research in cultural institutes, while others were working in retirement or in their spare time. They included such eminent people as Shen Yinmo (pp. 67–73), Qi Baishi, who was more widely known as a painter than a calligrapher, and Ye Gongchuo (pp. 74–9), the former Nationalist Party politician who had returned to China from Hong Kong in 1949.

Although these scholar-calligraphers continued to produce impressive works of art, the political hostility towards the elitist nature of their art made them cautious about the ideas they expressed (fig. 37). They were no longer willing to display publicly their favourite poems, regardless of whether they were their own or had been written by other poets. Indeed, many decided that it was better to be seen writing only poems or slogans in praise of 'New China' (often relying on classical idioms to lend authority to their message), or to copy out the poems of the much-respected leftist writer Lu Xun (1881–1936) or the words of the 'Socialist Internationale'. Such

politically acceptable works were often put on public display, and occasionally they were shown in group exhibitions.

Despite these constraints, Mao wanted no one to be in any doubt that he continued to regard calligraphy as an art form, although not necessarily a high-profile one. When the minister of culture, Zheng Zhenduo, declared in the early 1950s that calligraphy was just a script, Mao responded quickly. In the rather elliptical way in which he often chose to express himself, he said that he did not think it mattered whether China kept one more art. He also gave a modest amount of practical support to the art. In the late 1950s and early 1960s Mao agreed to the establishment of calligraphy research associations in both Beijing and Shanghai. More importantly, he allowed the Party's youth league to arrange for distinguished calligraphers to teach young enthusiasts at its own 'Youth Palaces'.

Making their mark

The new Chinese Government's restoration of the country's dilapidated major monuments provided opportunities for a number of calligraphers, as many of their inscriptions had to be replaced. One of the largest pieces of calligraphy commissioned at this time was the plaque for the Da Xiong Bao Dian, the main pavilion at Hangzhou's famous Lingyin Temple (fig. 38).

In China it was not only professional calligraphers who had written the large name plaques for palaces, temples and monuments; emperors had done so, too. And Mao did more of this kind of work than any former ruler. Although *The People's Daily* carried (as it does to this day) the calligraphic masthead he had provided in 1946, little of Mao's calligraphy was visible in public places in the early years of the new regime. By the late 1950s, however, it was to be seen on several of the capital's prominent new monuments and public buildings, most notably the Martyrs' Memorial, focal point of the newly enlarged Tiananmen Square, completed in 1958. Mao usually wrote these pieces in running script, breaking with the tradition of using regular or seal script for name plaques and inscriptions. Copies of some of Mao's political slogans were also on sale for display in offices and homes. They bore exhortations ranging from 'Increase Production' and 'Study Marxism-Leninism' to the more chilling 'Struggle'.

Mao's calligraphy was greatly prized and much solicited. By displaying an original piece of his work, one not only laid claim to some personal link with the Chairman, but by the same token gained some protection from the seemingly endless political campaigns and intrigues. Ye Gongchuo, one of Mao's scholar-calligrapher companions, prominently displayed in his house a letter that Mao had written to him. And although Guo Moruo (pp. 80–90), unquestionably the most prolific public calligrapher, had himself received personal letters from Mao, so keen was he to secure and display a really good example of his calligraphy that he actually kept a piece which Mao had asked him to give to someone else.

Despite the high regard in which Mao was held by his colleagues, they never invited him to provide the calligraphic titles for such institutions as 'The Chinese Communist Party', 'The People's Republic of China', 'The State Council' or the building on Tiananmen Square known as 'The Great Hall of the People'. It seems they felt that no individual should ever have the right to personalize these great institutions.

Other leading Chinese figures of the day often provided the calligraphy for the name plaques or titles of those institutions and publications with which they were closely associated. Among those written by Premier Zhou Enlai were the ones for China's international airline and the Beijing Hotel (where government leaders hosted receptions in the early years of the new regime). Many Chinese were privately amused by the fact that the head of the secret police, Kang Sheng – that great excavator of information – had provided the first masthead for the journal *Archaeology*. Further down the chain of command, provincial Party secretaries and governors were also keen to put inscriptions on their projects.

38 The name plaque for the Da Xiong Bao Dian pavilion was redone by Sha Menghai in 1955 and then again in 1986, with the characters written from right to left.

The prolific public calligrapher Guo Moruo was President of the Academy of Sciences. In the capital he created the name plaques for the restored Forbidden City, the adjoining park of Coal Hill and the Summer Palace. He also provided the calligraphy for China's best-known institution overseas, the Bank of China. Guo wrote the name plaque for the London branch of the bank when it moved to new premises in 1963. This calligraphic rendering was then adopted by the institution as a whole and was soon widely displayed in Hong Kong, where the Bank of China has many branches.

Political calligraphy

The modernization of China itself soon began to pose a long-term threat to the art of calligraphy. In the early 1950s the use of the fountain pen became fashionable for city officials. When teams from the Writers' Union were sent to help promote literacy in rural areas in 1956, a cartoon showed them with not only calligraphy brushes, but also pens.

The political atmosphere in China became somewhat more relaxed in 1956 when Mao declared that the time had come to let the people put forward their honest views about the performance of the new regime. This period became known as the 'Hundred Flowers Movement', a name taken from an ancient couplet (fig. 39). In keeping with the spirit of the time, Guo Moruo wrote out this couplet, together with a more socialist one. The two couplets were engraved on the wooden pillars in the private courtyard at Rong Bao Zhai (the 300-year-old shop in Beijing where leading artists congregated and for which Guo had earlier written the name plaque):

> *Let a hundred flowers bloom,*
> > *let a hundred schools of thought contend.*
> *The will of the masses becomes a tower of strength;*
> > *together they can achieve feats otherwise impossible.*

At first, people were reluctant to express their views. After a few months, however, the initial trickle of opinions had swelled to a torrent of criticism, mostly expressed in the form of 'big-character posters'. These were written out with a brush in large characters, on sheets of paper the size of a newspaper page, or bigger (fig. 40). The large brushes gave the people a power that the small fountain pen could not, especially in a society where they did not have easy access either to the media or to printing presses where their posters could be reproduced. There were historical precedents for large handwritten posters, but never before had they been used so prolifically.

The Party was shocked by the vehemence of the criticism it received. It responded swiftly by rounding up the critics and condemning them as

39 This cartoon reflects the belief of many artists and writers that the 'Hundred Flowers Movement' would open up a new era of artistic freedom.

40 After the Hundred Flowers Movement, Mao wanted to ensure that big-character posters were used to support his policies, rather than criticize them.

'Rightists'. Most were then either thrown out of their jobs or sent to the countryside for 'reform through labour'. Many professors of Chinese classics and Chinese literature lost their posts, even if they had not been unduly critical of the Party. From having been central to Chinese education they were all of a sudden regarded as expendable on the grounds that they represented 'Old China'. Not surprisingly, few students now chose to study these subjects. As a result, China began to cut itself off from the extra-ordinarily rich heritage of classical poetry that had nourished the art of calligraphy for more than two thousand years.

In the late 1950s calligraphy began to assume an even greater importance for Mao. As his colleagues sought to marginalize his role, he began to prepare his counterattack. Both Mao's poetry and his calligraphy played key roles in this process. In 1962 the appearance of his poem *Mount Liupan* took people by surprise. It had been created in a new and dramatic form of wild cursive calligraphy that he had been practising in private for the previous year (fig. 41). More than ever before, people now felt that Mao's distinctive style of calligraphy showed him to be a truly great leader. Over the next three years he published further poems in this style.

In the summer of 1966 Mao unleashed the 'Great Proletarian Cultural Revolution', an evocative title that carried with it a more destructive sense

发扬民主作风
坚持群众路线

than the later simplified version, 'The Cultural Revolution'. Its ostensible aim was to 'smash the Four Olds': old thought, old culture, old customs, old practice. Students were mobilized to act as the 'Red Guards' who would carry out this task. Mao's real aim, however, was to overthrow those in the Party hierarchy and throughout the establishment who, he believed, were opposed to him.

From the very beginning of the Cultural Revolution the Red Guards, under the careful guidance of Mao's henchmen, made use of big-character posters to vilify Mao's opponents. Then, on 5 August 1966, Mao called upon the Red Guards to 'Bombard the Headquarters' of the Party. This exhortation was widely promoted by an illustration of Mao holding a large brush, coloured blood-red in some versions, accompanied by the words: 'My first big-character poster' (fig. 42).

The violence that followed Mao's call to action soon ran out of control. Across the country tens of millions of posters were pasted up. They exhibited the largest collection of lies and slanders ever publicly displayed in history.

Despite the revolutionary chaos that raged, Mao's entourage still managed to uphold many of the standards of Old China. The small number of officials who remained in the Party Secretariat continued to prepare reports for Mao that were beautifully written with a brush, because everyone knew that this was what Mao expected of them.

At the top, erudition was still applauded. On 13 September 1971, Premier Zhou Enlai and his senior colleagues waited nervously for news

41 The enlarged facsimile of Mao's poem *Mount Liupan* that was displayed in Shanghai Airport until 1995, when it was removed to make way for new duty-free shops.

炮 打 司 令 部
（我 的 一 张 大 字 报 ）

全国第一张马列主义的大字报和人民日报评论员的评论，写
得何等好呵，请同志们重读一遍这张大字报和这个评论。可是在
五十多天里，从中央到地方的某些领导同志，却反其道而行之，站
在反动的资产阶级立场上，实行资产阶级专政，将无产阶级轰轰
烈烈的文化大革命运动打下去，颠倒是非，混淆黑白，围剿革命
派，压制不同意见，实行白色恐怖，自以为得意，长资产阶级的
威风，灭无产阶级的志气，又何其毒也，联系到一九六二年的右
倾和一九六四年形"左"而实右的错误倾向，岂不是可以发人深醒
的吗；

毛泽东

42 Following Mao's call to 'Bombard the Headquarters', there was a dramatic upsurge in the use of big-character posters.

of the aeroplane on which Lin Biao, Mao's chosen successor, had fled from China towards the Soviet Union. When they heard that it had crashed in Mongolia, Qiao Guanhua, the deputy foreign minister, responded by composing a poem based on one by a famous Tang dynasty poet about a rebel tribe that had fled north after an unsuccessful attempt on the emperor's life. On the spot Qiao reworked the words to match the events of the Lin Biao affair, succeeding in keeping the original rhyme. His colleagues thought the result so brilliant that Qiao was asked to write it down with a brush on fine paper. He then gave the calligraphy to Zhou Enlai, who framed it and hung it on his wall.

Among the Red Guards, standards were not as high (fig. 43). The calligraphy of many of them was so poor that the main art-publishing houses received permission to print booklets on how to write good basic calligraphy. The texts were based on Mao's writings and poems, but in each case they were written out following the style of one of several great calligraphers of the past. For example, the script of Ouyang Xun (557–641) was used as a model for the writing of clear, regular characters, while that of Yan Zhenqing (709–785) helped aspiring calligraphers to write large characters. Millions of copies of these booklets were sold. In these inauspicious circumstances, old cultural values were already beginning to reassert themselves.

After two chaotic years of Cultural Revolution, large numbers of Red Guards were sent from the cities to the countryside to 'learn from labouring together with the masses'. Most of them felt isolated and dejected so far

49

from home, and resented the fact that they were unable to continue their education. To allay their misery, many of them began to study calligraphy. To avoid criticism, however, they would practise writing out the *Thoughts of Chairman Mao* from booklets of the type mentioned above. In some cases, as in that of Sa Benjie (pp. 216–25), it was possible to obtain first-rate coaching from experienced calligraphers who had also been banished to the countryside.

As the turmoil and violence lessened at the beginning of the 1970s, China sought to improve its ties with those countries that shared a hostility towards its arch-enemy, the Soviet Union. This shift in policy paved the way for the visit to China of President Nixon and Dr Henry Kissinger, his National Security Adviser, in February 1972. Later the same year, China made another important diplomatic breakthrough, this time with Japan.

43 This little Red Guard's calligraphy was good enough to impress illiterate farmers. Many of the older Red Guards, however, recognized that well-written big-character posters attracted the widest attention.

The restoration of full diplomatic relations between China and Japan (for the first time since the 1930s) provided Guo Moruo with an opportunity to obtain political support for calligraphy again to be treated as an art in China. Premier Zhou Enlai accepted Guo's recommendation that the magazine *People's China* should celebrate the occasion by publishing the works of contemporary Japanese and Chinese calligraphers.

One of the pieces selected by the Chinese side was a rendering by Lin Sanzhi (pp. 140–5) of Mao's famous poem that begins with the very appropriate line, 'A new dawn breaks in the East' (see pp. 106–7). When Guo Moruo first saw Lin's piece, he was so excited by it that he declared it the finest work of calligraphy to have been produced in China in the past 300 years. Although Guo's view was not universally shared, his statement made people believe that it was once again respectable to take an interest in the art of calligraphy.

The publication of these works did not result in the cultural thaw for which so many had hoped. When Premier Zhou was hospitalized with cancer at the end of 1973, Mao's wife Jiang Qing and her associates – later known as the 'Gang of Four' – intensified their efforts to overthrow the moderates. She staged an exhibition of 2,311 so-called 'black works of art' to show the Chinese people what was unacceptable in contemporary art. In essence, Jiang Qing was following a practice established in Nazi Germany of branding certain types of art as inherently 'degenerate'.

One of the pieces Jiang Qing singled out for vehement criticism was a huge horizontal panel of calligraphy by Li Luogong (pp. 125–31; fig. 44). It was an extremely bold work, based on early Chinese pictograms but executed with the extraordinary vitality of an artist who had closely studied the work of the group of French painters known as the Fauves ('Wild Beasts'). The piece bore the words of Mao's poem that begins 'I lost my proud poplar', which he had written about the loss of his first wife. Jiang Qing certainly hated Li's piece on stylistic grounds, but one suspects that she also hated it because it was about Mao's first wife. Hopes of an early renaissance of Chinese art and calligraphy suddenly evaporated.

On 8 January 1976, Premier Zhou Enlai died. Two weeks later, in the privacy of his study, Guo Moruo wrote out a poem that expressed the sense of despair and sadness of all those people who had so admired Zhou and who had such a deep affection for him. The last lines read as follows:

Neither the vastness of the heavens,
nor all the expanse of the earth
are enough to bury your greatness.

Despite this widespread sentiment – indeed, because of it – the Gang of Four denied the people any public opportunity to express their grief over Zhou's death. But three months later, during the festival of Qing Ming, when the Chinese traditionally honour the dead, huge crowds poured spontaneously into Tiananmen Square to pay homage to Zhou's memory.

On the ledge of the Martyrs' Memorial, right in the centre of the square, a group from the Chinese Academy of Sciences erected four tall panels of calligraphy for all to see (fig. 45). They bore the words of an unsigned allegorical poem, which, in effect, declared that the Gang of Four's days were numbered. Before long about a million people had crowded into the square and the adjoining streets. As a sign of mourning, they carried hundreds of thousands of white paper flowers, which seemed to fill up the whole of the square. The mood became increasingly defiant as people declaimed poems they had written praising the Premier and criticizing the Gang of Four. After a few days the police succeeded in clearing the square, bringing to an end the greatest public protest the Gang of Four had ever faced.

Within the intelligentsia some people soon became bold enough to share the hatred they felt for the Gang of Four with their friends through the medium of erudite poems and prose. Since even these 'coded' messages were extremely dangerous, should they fall into the wrong hands, the recipients would always destroy the paper on which they were written immediately after reading them.

Mao died in September 1976, having inflicted grievous damage on China. His collectivization of agriculture and the ill-conceived dash to boost industrial production during the Great Leap Forward of 1958–60 had transformed poor harvests into a terrible famine that had killed millions. Then his 'Great Proletarian Cultural Revolution' had shattered many of the achievements of New China. Tens of thousands of good citizens had been murdered or driven to suicide, and millions had suffered at the hands of the mob. Living standards had again fallen, and the Party had come close to destroying itself.

A month after Mao's death, the Gang of Four were arrested. Calligraphers and scholars were now free to write out publicly the powerful pieces condemning the Gang of Four which earlier they had shared only with their friends (fig. 46).

In 1977 Mao's embalmed body was placed in the Chairman Mao Memorial Hall that had just been completed at the southern end of Tiananmen Square. The calligraphy installed above the entrance to this undistinguished piece of architecture was by Hua Guoteng, the new Chairman

45 Mao's first big-character poster (fig. 42) gave a violent impetus to the Cultural Revolution. Four panels of calligraphy on the Martyrs' Memorial helped bring it to an end.

46 In 1977 Huang Miaozi rewrote a piece he had first composed after people flocked to Tiananmen Square in 1976. The sense of his couplet is:

*A hundred thousand wild flowers
   have been scattered, as in a dream.
Now the will of the people, with the
   elemental force of wind and thunder,
   shall determine China's fate.*

of the Chinese Communist Party and a man whose calligraphy did not attract the admiration he would have wished.

China begins to open up

After a decade of turbulence, China needed to heal the wounds which the Cultural Revolution had inflicted on society and get the economy moving once again. In the late 1970s Deng Xiaoping, who had suffered badly at Mao's hands during the Cultural Revolution, re-emerged as China's pre-eminent leader. He soon forged ahead with bold new policies aimed at promoting economic reform and the opening-up of China's relations with the outside world.

Alongside the reforms and the relaxation of restrictions, there was an upsurge of activity in painting and calligraphy. For the first time since the early 1960s, books about Western art could be purchased in China. There were exhibitions of Western art in Beijing and Shanghai, and dozens of Chinese artists were allowed to travel overseas. Western styles of painting were avidly copied, and paintings of female nudes were seen in China for the first time since the 1940s.

The change in the political atmosphere provided Professor Zhang Ding, President of the Central Academy of Design, with a welcome opportunity to press for calligraphy to be revitalized. To this end, he argued, calligraphers should draw upon the lessons to be learned from both Western and Chinese art. Zhang Ding's views carried weight not only because of his influential position as head of the Academy, but also because he enjoyed the rare distinction of being the only Chinese painter from the People's Republic of China to have met Pablo Picasso (fig. 47).

Calligraphy soon became more popular than ever before. Since the end of the Cultural Revolution, many people had turned to calligraphy in the hope of finding solace in the calm repetition of its exercises. Then, in 1981, the authorities took the lead in setting up a Chinese Calligraphers' Association, the first such nationwide body ever to be established in the country. Membership fees were usually paid in cash and the Association had to buy two machines to count up the huge influx of banknotes.

The Association's appointed chairman was Shu Tong, a respected veteran of the Communist Party to whom Mao had paid the back-handed compliment of describing him as the best calligrapher in the Red Army. Because of his background, however, Shu Tong was able to persuade people that it was now acceptable to engage themselves publicly in the art. His three vice-chairmen – Qi Gong, Sha Menghai and Chen Shuliang – were all renowned scholar-calligraphers.

Within a few years, hundreds of thousands of calligraphy enthusiasts had enrolled for the Association's provincial activities across the country, with the top few thousand belonging to the body at national level. Calligraphy exhibitions and competitions soon became fashionable at all levels; some were devoted to the works of children, others to those of university students, retired officials and senior citizens (fig. 57). At times, public interest in such events was so intense that crowds would force their way into exhibition halls before opening time in their eagerness to see who had been awarded prizes. Several people who have become well known in the world of calligraphy first came to prominence though the awards they won in these early competitions – for example, Wang Dongling, Wang Nanming, Qiu Zhenzhong and Zhang Yiguo.

However, the impact of the Cultural Revolution on calligraphy was all too apparent. Among the young there was an overall absence of good technique, scant knowledge of the classics, and certainly no ability to write clever variants of classical poems. One positive note was that some of the young adults who had learnt to write big-character posters during the Cultural Revolution had developed a much freer style than could be achieved by the older, classically trained calligraphers.

Both inside and outside the new Chinese Calligraphers' Association there were still artists, such as Sha Menghai, Qi Gong and Lin Sanzhi, who could produce classical works in the grand tradition of Chinese calligraphy. There was also a great deal of work available to keep good calligraphers busy. They were invited to rewrite the calligraphy for the name plaques and other inscriptions at the thousands of cultural monuments that had been damaged by Red Guards or neglected during the Cultural Revolution. Most calligraphers were also able to publish books about their work and to sell the originals to local customers and foreign visitors.

At this time Japanese calligraphy became highly influential. It had been exhibited in China in 1957, 1958, 1962 and 1978, but it was not until the 1980s that many Chinese calligraphers were able to visit Japan and see for themselves how the Japanese had transformed the art during the post-war period. Several leading Chinese artists adopted the Japanese style of concentrating more on visual aesthetics than on content, but a number of others, including those in the Modernist movement, felt that the Japanese approach to calligraphy was rather superficial. They therefore preferred to draw on what they saw as the uniquely Chinese elements of calligraphy in their efforts to revitalize the art.

By the mid-1980s certain artists wanted to push calligraphy much further forward than the Japanese had done. Most of them were not

47 During his meeting with Zhang Ding in Paris in 1956, Picasso remarked that, had he been born Chinese, he would have been a calligrapher, not a painter.

calligraphers by training, nor were they young, but they all felt that the time had come for change. The Modernist movement began to emerge.

In 1985 Huang Miaozi, Gu Gan, Li Luogong and others held China's very first exhibition of Modernist calligraphy. Somewhat to their surprise, the authorities agreed that it could be staged in the China Art Gallery in Beijing. The exhibition attracted huge crowds and aroused a great deal of controversy – not unlike the Armory Show, the well-known exhibition of European art held in New York City in 1913, which introduced Cubism to America (most notoriously in the form of Marcel Duchamp's *Nude descending a Staircase*). Many visitors simply could not understand what the Modernists were doing, and those who did were either delighted or outraged to see so many long-standing conventions being flouted (fig. 48).

While the Modernist movement was finding its feet, many other experiments were also taking place. Zhang Dawo (pp. 227–35) was creating works in which the characters looked like three-dimensional sculptures of the ideas they were intended to convey. Wang Dongling (pp. 163–71) was producing massive pieces of calligraphy with an unprecedented energy and freedom of movement that reflected the sense of artistic liberation he had achieved during the Cultural Revolution (fig. 50). His combination of Western and Chinese images in calligraphic collages was a novel innovation.

Even before the Modernist school had fully gathered momentum, the first shoots of the Avant-Garde movement were beginning to sprout. The unrelenting official disapproval of abstract art in China led certain artists to argue that it should be acceptable, since calligraphy itself could be considered an abstract art form. One of these protesters was the young calligrapher Bai Qianshen (b. 1955). In 1981 he sought to put the point across by writing eight seemingly authentic Chinese characters, which were in fact wholly unreadable (fig. 49). People to whom he showed them automatically attempted to read them in the normal way, just as if they were rarely used characters which they did not immediately recognize. Bai's experiment opened up the way for others to exploit the same idea.

By the late 1980s the general optimism that had marked the earlier part of the decade was beginning to fade. Resentment was directed at bureaucrats known to be profiteering from the reforms, and calls were made for political reform. The popular ditties of the time were savage, explicit and out of keeping with the tone of this book. Nevertheless, it was against this background that the Avant-Garde movement emerged in 1988.

Whereas the Modernists had been influenced by twentieth-century Western artists such as Picasso, Matisse and Klee, the young artists of the Avant-Garde tended to be much more inspired by the Abstract Expressionism of the 1950s and 1960s and by contemporary Western art. One particularly seminal experience was the 1985 exhibition in Beijing of

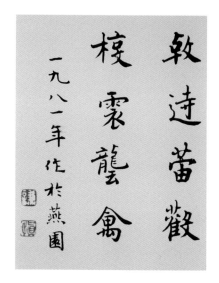

49 In 1981 Bai Qianshen was the first calligrapher to write formal Chinese 'characters' that could not be read.

50 In his work *Mount Tai* (1987) Wang Dongling used a poem by Ruan Ji (210–263) to evoke the grandeur of China's landscape, by imagining what one might see looking down from Heaven. Its sense is that:

*The towering Mount Tai looks as small as a grindstone,
while the mighty Yellow River snakes its way across the land like a silken cord.*

Robert Rauschenberg's paintings, collages, photographs, videos and installations. Despite the enormous differences between American and Chinese culture, the exhibition seems to have appealed to a widely shared sense of unease with, and alienation from, modern society. At the same time, Chinese artists were keen to learn more about some of the experimental calligraphy being produced in Taiwan and the United States.

The Avant-Garde has remained controversial ever since its emergence in 1988. It began with the dramatic installation work *Books from Heaven* by Xu Bing (b. 1955), which was made up of thousands of volumes of traditional woodblock-printed books full of unreadable characters (fig. 51). Few people regarded the work as a simple play on the well-known Chinese concept that Heaven had first given mankind characters that could only be understood by those with divine powers. Most saw Xu Bing's intent for what it was: to present a powerful negation of Chinese bureaucracy, history and literature. His installation was all the more an affront to Chinese culture because China prides itself on having the longest continuously used system of writing in the world.

The cross-currents in Chinese culture

The mass demonstrations that took place in Tiananmen Square in 1989 highlighted the influence that modern media were already having on communications in China. While many demonstrators proclaimed their views on calligraphic banners, others felt that their point could be made more effectively through the use of symbols, such as the 'Goddess of Democracy', on placards written in English, which had the potential to reach an international audience.

Following the suppression of the demonstrations on 4 June 1989, there was a political clampdown. Economic reform came to a standstill and China's links with the outside world were sharply curtailed. This reaction was relatively short-lived, however. In 1992 Deng Xiaoping called for his policies to be relaunched and with greater vigour, declaring that 'to be rich is to be glorious'. His economic reforms attracted investment from overseas and China's economy began to flourish, especially in the coastal regions. Foreign consumer goods, often backed by slick Western advertising, started to flood into the country. Perhaps not surprisingly, a by-product of this economic boom was a new lease of life for Chinese calligraphy.

In some respects, New China began to look more and more like Old China. New civic infrastructure projects, commercial buildings, organizations, companies, hotels, shops, restaurants, magazines and television programmes all needed name plaques or titles. Most of them were provided by calligraphers, but a large number were produced by national or local political leaders who had played a role in the development of these new projects or businesses.

In Shanghai, for example, the first two bridges that were built across the river to the newly developed area of Pudong carry huge name plaques written in the calligraphy of Deng Xiaoping, who backed the development of the region. The name plaque on the Oriental Pearl TV Tower – the symbol of modern Shanghai – was created by President Jiang Zemin, who was Party Secretary in the city during the inauguration of the project. Since becoming President, Jiang Zemin has created many more inscriptions (fig. 52).

The market for calligraphy has also been fuelled by an increase in the number of new private buyers – some acquiring the calligraphy for themselves and others purchasing pieces as gifts for their contacts in business or government. A notable amount of calligraphy has also been bought by

visitors to China, especially Overseas Chinese. The combination of tenured positions in art colleges and the ability to sell their works in a relatively buoyant market has enabled some of China's best calligraphers to enjoy comfortable lifestyles.

Some of the disagreeable side-effects of reform have tainted the name of calligraphy. For example, the Hunan Provincial Calligraphers' Association got into trouble for charging people more than US$1,000 to become a member and US$12,000 to become a vice-president of the organization, knowing full well that these titles were being used largely to boost the social standing of the individuals concerned. Even worse, a provincial vice-governor was recently executed for accepting bribes. He had managed to hide his ill-gotten gains by claiming that he had received very large payments for his – it must be said – excellent calligraphy.

By the mid-1990s the calligraphy of many people in China had been seriously afflicted by what one might call the 'curse of the ball-point pen'. To make matters worse, that of the younger generation was rapidly being impaired by the widespread use of computers. Handwritten calligraphy was also in decline in the commercial sector. More and more of the pieces created for shop signs and advertising were produced by computer and not by the brush. At the same time, the use of Western-style graphics, images and logos increased.

A much more serious challenge to the state of modern calligraphy in China has been the toll that time has taken on the leading exponents of the Grand Tradition. By the early 1990s most of the great calligraphers whose careers had stretched back into the traditional culture prevailing prior to 1949 had passed away. As this book goes to press, the best-known survivor is Qi Gong (fig. 53), who was elevated to the chairmanship of the Chinese Calligraphers' Association in 1992 and became honorary chairman in 1996.

Although many people lament the passing of the Grand Tradition, no one seriously believes that in the twenty-first century the possibility exists to regenerate the cultural refinement and erudition that would be needed to sustain it. However, Neo-Classical artists are creating works that appeal to those, both young and old, who yearn to be led along a more accessible path into the complex pleasures of Chinese culture.

Examples of Neo-Classical calligraphy can regularly be seen on display in China, either in group exhibitions or in one-man (and occasionally one-woman) shows. In both Shanghai and Beijing there are dozens of such exhibitions every year. In addition, in each of the major cities there are shops that specialize in selling Classical and Neo-Classical calligraphy.

The Modernists continue to experiment with the creation of calligraphic pieces that are much more like paintings than traditional calligraphy. These works, however, are still based on characters that can be read, albeit at times with difficulty. During the 1990s the output of such artists became much bolder, largely a result of the art they had seen in Europe, the United States and Australia.

54 In his Mouton Rothschild label Gu Gan intermingled five different forms of the character for 'heart', to symbolize the links between mankind across the five continents.

Encre de Chine par Gu Gan

"Cœur à Cœur"

1996

toute la récolte a été mise en bouteilles au Château

Philippine de Rothschild

Château

Mouton Rothschild®

PAUILLAC

APPELLATION PAUILLAC CONTROLÉE

Baronne Philippine de Rothschild g. f. a.

PRODUCE OF FRANCE   PROPRIETAIRE

A major indication of the growing international interest in Modernist calligraphy came in 1998, when Château Mouton Rothschild invited Gu Gan to design the label for its 1996 vintage (fig. 54), an honour previously accepted by some of the greatest Western artists, including Picasso and Matisse. Although the influence of Western art can still often be seen in Modernist works, many artists feel that the future success of Modernism depends on its remaining rooted in Chinese culture.

After its dramatic emergence in the late 1980s, the Avant-Garde movement soon found itself in difficulty as it struggled to create a distinctive form of calligraphy. At exhibitions in Shanghai and Nanjing in 1991,

Wang Nanming (pp. 250–5) and Zhang Qiang (pp. 256–63) produced works devoid of meaning, which were intended to challenge popular assumptions about the nature of calligraphy and the way it is used in Chinese society. The following year Wang produced his famous video work *Combination: Balls of Characters* (fig. 55).

The Avant-Garde soon became engaged in a heated debate as to whether it was possible to have an art called calligraphy in which the characters were meaningless. In 1995, however, Zhang Qiang had some success in reframing the debate. He argued that if a painting without a representational image can still be a painting, then calligraphy without readable characters can still be calligraphy. He pointed out that it was possible to create effects with Chinese brushes, inks and papers that could not be matched by those used in Western art. Even unreadable calligraphy could strike deep cultural chords and make statements conveying an artist's views about the age in which he was working.

In 1999 a major exhibition called the 'Retrospective of Chinese Modern Calligraphy at the End of the Twentieth Century' was staged in Chengdu, the capital of Sichuan province in western China. The local governor opened the exhibition to demonstrate Sichuan's enthusiasm for all things modern. Some of the visitors supported the assertion of one critic that the event was 'the last insurrection in Chinese contemporary art this century', but others did not. They felt that more needed to be done to reflect modern Chinese society and the issues faced by people today. Yang Yingshi, an art editor of *The China Daily*, suggested that the way forward for modern calligraphy was to make a more determined effort to question the culture of the past and the present and to look to the future.

Since the early 1990s personal freedom in China has increased. A growing number of issues are discussed openly in public and people vent their feelings more freely in private. Within the confines of Beijing nightclubs, young women wearing miniskirts and studded leather collars sing songs that are renowned for their biting critiques of life in modern China. Many calligraphers express their views with equal impact, but they do so to a different audience, by selecting quotes from the respected classics and then exploiting the rich ambiguities inherent in the Chinese language (see, for example, Qi Gong, Han Yu, Gu Gan, Huang Miaozi).

Not all calligraphy, of course, is concerned with social commentary or existential meditation. Indeed, calligraphers often aim to transport their audience along the beautiful traces of their brushwork into the serenity of elegant language, or, by the use of more dramatic effects, to excite the senses (fig. 56).

55 Wang Nanming has created a whole new artistic vocabulary with his use of paper balls.

Calligraphy in the twenty-first century

56 In his 'flying white' paintings Zhang Dawo seeks to re-create the pleasure, insecurity and excitement encountered in dreams.

In the past twenty-five years China has been transformed. So, too, has Chinese calligraphy: while it remains a means of communication, it is now seen primarily as an art form. Over the next fifty years the pressures driving change in China will be just as great as in the recent past. The interplay of economic reform, social change and political development will be complex. No one can know what will emerge. But within these broad changes are signs of the factors likely to affect the future development of calligraphy. One of the most important is the severance of the link between it and the ruling elite. People at the the top no longer feel that their position requires them to excel at calligraphy. Indeed, it will be a pleasant surprise if one of China's future leaders does display a marked flair for calligraphy.

Already we have seen the end of another important tradition – that of the *literati* – as writers and poets on the one hand and calligraphers on the other have gone their separate ways. As standards of education continue to rise there will be greater literacy, but as education increasingly revolves around science, technology and economics, there will be fewer people who are truly knowledgeable about classical Chinese culture.

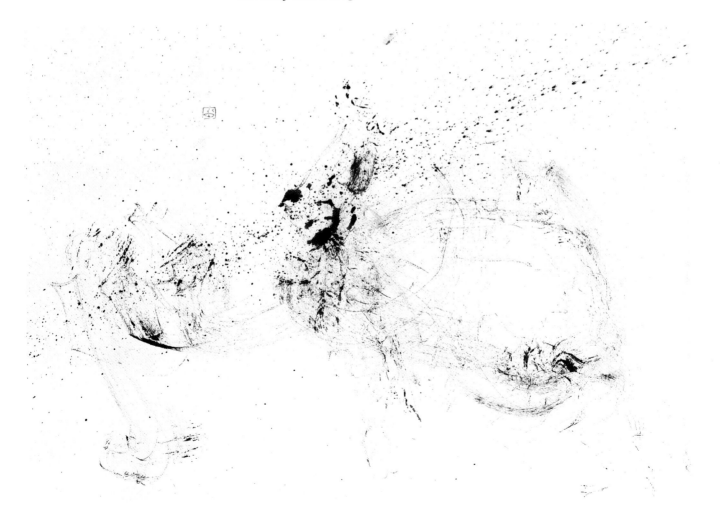

57 Geng Biao (b. 1906) went on the Long March with Mao. He struggled to educate himself, rose through the ranks of the Party and was appointed to the Politburo in 1977. After retiring in 1982, he took up calligraphy. In 1995 he presented the author with this evocation of summer, which reads: 'The song of the birds and the scent of the flowers.'

58 Many of the young people taking extra lessons in calligraphy outside of school achieve a high standard.

This trend is following a pattern already well established in the West, but it has what might be called 'Chinese characteristics'. So great is the desire to be computer-literate that there has been a substantial decline in the number of children attending calligraphy classes after school. Another major problem is that people who write mainly by means of a keyboard soon forget how to write characters with a pen, let alone a brush.

Conversely, there are still many young people in China who aspire to write well with a brush, and the present relaxed atmosphere is encouraging the development of artistic talent. The Youth Palaces, and increasingly private tuition, still supplement the modest extent to which writing with a brush is taught in schools (fig. 58). At several art colleges calligraphy is now recognized as a subject in its own right and not merely as a branch of art in general. Both at the National Academy of Fine Arts in Hangzhou and at the Central Academy of Art in Beijing it is now possible to study for a doctorate in calligraphy. In addition, there are now numerous magazines and newspapers dealing with both traditional and modern calligraphy. Foreigners in China are also beginning to take more of an interest in learning Chinese calligraphy.

Currently there are literally thousands of young Chinese who are either receiving or have already received a good basic calligraphic education. The more talented among them will be well placed to explore the possibilities of Neo-Classicism, Modernism and the Avant-Garde.

However, the cultural climate in China is less conducive to artistic expression than that in North America or Europe. Some spectacles are acceptable, while others are not. Gu Wenda (b. 1955), for example, has been able to create pieces in the United States that he could never have displayed in China. But the experience of other countries, such as Russia in the late Imperial era and the first decades of the Soviet Union, suggests that sometimes it is from the narrower margins of freedom within which artists are allowed to operate that some of the best and most exciting work emerges.

As Gu Gan has often said, 'Chinese characters are abstract. Calligraphy, from the earliest times, has been grounded in abstract art.' Calligraphy is a vehicle that facilitates the creation of art which is not only deeply rooted in Chinese culture, but is also capable of striking a sympathetic chord with Western viewers. Given the developments of the past quarter of a century, we have every reason to expect that we shall see some further outstanding calligraphy coming out of China in the foreseeable future.

SHEN YINMO
1883–1971

Keeping the art alive

When the Communists came to power in 1949, Shen Yinmo was already regarded as one of China's most eminent calligraphers. He was then living in Shanghai, where Chen Yi – his great admirer – had just been appointed mayor. The patronage that Chen Yi bestowed upon Shen gave him a privileged position in Shanghai society that helped him to promote the art he loved most at a time when it was under increasing threat.

The patriotic reformer

After a traditional upbringing, Shen, like many other reform-minded young Chinese men of his day, went to study in Japan. In 1907, after more than two years at university there, he returned to China, where he taught at a school in his family's home town of Huzhou in Zhejiang province, the birthplace of the great calligrapher Zhao Mengfu (1254–1322).

While he was in Huzhou, Shen met Chen Duxiu, who was later to found the Chinese Communist Party. After becoming a professor of literature at Beijing University in 1913, Shen met many more progressive intellectuals in the New Culture Movement. He showed himself to be a keen advocate of more extensive use of the spoken language in literature and everyday written communication, and before long he was taken on as one of the editors of *New Youth*, the Movement's influential magazine. This publication played a key role in launching the 'May Fourth Movement' of 1919, which in turn provided a major impetus to reform in the early days of Republican China.

Even as a young man, Shen displayed remarkable talent as a calligrapher. He continued to work hard at developing his skills by practising writing at least 500 characters every morning before breakfast. With the opening of the Palace Museum to the public in the late 1920s, Shen had his first opportunity to study some of the finest pieces of calligraphy in existence. He was attracted to the fluid, graceful styles of Wang Xizhi (303–361), Wang Xianzhi (344–386), Chu Suiliang (596–658) and Mi Fu (1051–1107).

In 1932, just before reaching the age of fifty, Shen accepted the presidency of the newly established Peiping University in Beijing. Within months, however, he had resigned because he did not accept the University's ban on student protests. He decided to move south to the more liberal atmosphere of Shanghai, where he became director the Sino-French Cultural and Publishing Commission.

Shen's duties at the Commission were not onerous. He was able to devote considerable time to his calligraphy, studying especially the work of Chu Suiliang. Even at this stage his calligraphy was so praised for its elegance and versatility that he was the first person ever to be able to stage a one-man exhibition of his works in the city.

When the Japanese occupied the Chinese part of Shanghai in 1939, Shen moved to Chongqing, China's wartime capital, where he served as a member of the government's supervisory commission. As this position was little more than a sinecure, he had plenty of time in which to continue his research into the history and theory of calligraphy and to practise the art. In Chongqing he enjoyed the company of several distinguished calligraphers, including Yu Youren (1879–1964) and Guo Moruo (pp. 80–90), whom he had first met in Japan in 1921.

Shen's spirits were greatly raised by the arrival in Chongqing of Ms Chu Baoquan, who had been the prettiest girl on campus when he was teaching at Beijing University. Throughout the war the couple comforted each other, and their friendship blossomed into romance. After Japan's defeat, Shen moved from Chongqing back to Shanghai. There he acquired a three-storey terraced house in the Hongkou district, where he was to live for the rest of his life (the house is now a memorial museum). Soon afterwards he married Ms Chu. In this difficult period, however, he had trouble making a living from selling his calligraphy.

With the Communist takeover of Shanghai in 1949, Shen suddenly rose to prominence. He was the first of the city's leading intellectuals on whom Chen Yi called after becoming mayor of Shanghai. Shen was made deputy head of the city's new Cultural Administration Bureau and a member of

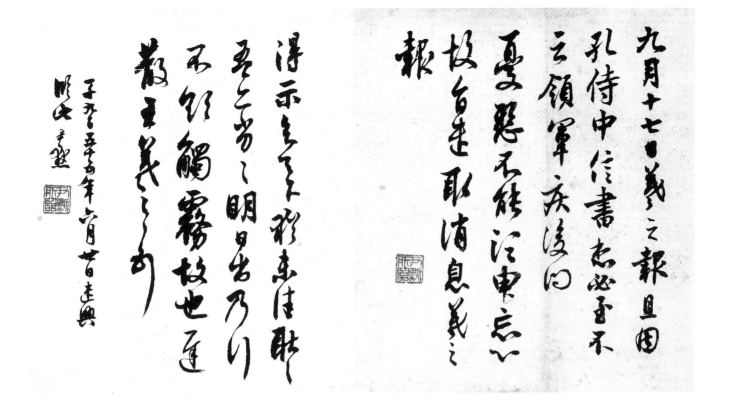

60, 61 Shen's copies of two of Wang Xizhi's famous short letters.

the People's Congress of the Shanghai Municipality. Then in 1956 he was appointed to the newly established Chinese People's Political Consultative Conference. More importantly, it was widely known in Shanghai that Chen Yi saw Shen frequently to discuss not only the new museum and library, but also their mutual interest in poetry and calligraphy.

Being very progressive in his political outlook, Shen was happy to write poems in support of the new regime: praising the workers, hailing major construction projects, and welcoming socialist ideals and the advent of the New China. These works remained deeply influenced by the classical tradition of which he was part. One of his favourite sources was the Song poet Lu You, whose views were also strongly patriotic. In addition, Shen genuinely admired the poems of Mao Zedong; he wrote them out often and published collections of his renderings of them. For his friends he would write out innocuous classical homilies such as: 'If you meet difficulty, you must deal with it yourself.'

The early 1950s were among Shen's happiest years. He and his wife were very close; every year on her birthday he gave her a romantic poem that he had written specially to mark the occasion. Their contentment with life was all the greater because, like other top scholars, Shen was paid 300 yuan a month, a huge sum in those days.

In his house in Shanghai, Shen surrounded himself with his favourite pieces of calligraphy and poetry – a selection that remained virtually un-changed until the Cultural Revolution. It included two pieces in regular script that were his copies of masterpieces from the Sui (589–618) and Tang (618–906) dynasties, a poem he had written about his home town of Huzhou whilst living in Chongqing during the war, a rendering in his own calligraphy of Mao Zedong's stirring poem *The Loushan Pass* (one of Shen's favourites) and one of the birthday poems he had given to his wife.

A classical innovator

Although deeply influenced by the classical traditions of calligraphy, Shen was an innovator. Since the 1930s he had been one of the main champions of the movement to revive interest in the lighter styles of running script and cursive script, on the basis of manuscripts that had been written between the fourth and thirteenth centuries.

From his parallel study of the works of Zhao Mengfu, Shen learned how to write much larger characters in cursive script. He even produced a pair of scrolls three metres long, with each character perfectly proportioned and balanced. In his late years he was particularly keen to re-create the elegance of the large characters that had been prevalent during the Six Dynasties (265–589). One of his most striking pieces consisted of the two large characters *zao ji*, which mean 'creating the ultimate'.

Few twentieth-century calligraphers have matched Shen's skill in using a brush. He had a masterful knowledge of the qualities of different types of brushes, of mixes of ink and water, and above all of the effects that could be achieved by changing the speed, pressure and direction of the brush. His understanding of ink and brush enabled him to imbue his work with a rare delicacy of tone (see fig. 19, p. 27). Shen once said of Chinese calligraphy that 'without sound, it has the rhythm of music; without colour, it acquires the beauty of painting'. His own work bears out that description and was widely admired for seeming to dance across the paper.

These skills are reflected in a rendering he did 'for pleasure' in 1955 of two pieces by the calligrapher he had come to admire the most, Wang Xizhi. No original calligraphy by Wang has survived, but among the few good copies of his work were two short letters that had been in Japan since the seventh century. The publication of facsimiles of them in 1954 had aroused much excitement among devotees of Wang's calligraphy in China. The letters read as follows:

> *On the 17th of the 9th month, from Wang Xizhi.*
> *Since Secretary Kong's letter should be arriving, I don't want someone*
>   *else to ask about it. But as I'm worried, I am writing to ask you*
>   *if it has arrived.*

Details of fig. 60

I have received your letter. I have heard that you are not feeling well;
nor am I. I shall go tomorrow, after the sun is up, as I don't want
to be in the fog or mist.

The lack of import in the letters' content is more than compensated for by the extraordinary quality of their brushwork, which Shen captured beautifully in his rendering of them (figs 60 and 61), despite claiming to have copied them out 'in an idle moment'.

Promoting calligraphy

Although deeply romantic in his private life, Shen displayed a steely determination when it came to maintaining the highest standards of classical calligraphy. In 1955 he was instrumental in the setting up of the Shanghai Chinese Painting Academy, of which he served as the first director. Despite the fact that calligraphy was not mentioned in the Academy's title, Shen made quite sure that the subject was taught there.

As director, he decided that the best way to obtain further support for the venture was to exploit the Chinese leadership's interest in improving relations with Japan, now a close military ally of the US and a country with which China had no diplomatic relations. As a distinguished calligrapher who had studied in Japan, Shen was one of the few figures (along with Guo Moruo) who could help influence Japanese opinion through the improvement of cultural relations between the two nations.

The Japanese calligraphy that was exhibited in China in 1957 and 1958 made much Chinese calligraphy look rather mundane in comparison. This led Shen to insist that if China was to exploit calligraphy effectively in terms of improving its relations with Japan, then Chinese calligraphers and scholars of the art would need the same high degree of official backing as was enjoyed by their Japanese counterparts.

In 1960 Chen Yi (who by then had become China's foreign minister) took the matter up with Mao Zedong, and soon Shen was made head of the new Shanghai Calligraphy and Seal Carving Research Association. Mao had recognized that something needed to be done, but for political reasons did not wish to give the art of calligraphy too much prominence. It was for this reason that he had accepted the establishment of a 'research association', but stopped short of creating an institute in Shanghai, let alone a national one.

Shen's already high standing in China's art world continued to rise. In 1960 Premier Zhou Enlai appointed him deputy director of the Central Academy of Culture and History, an honour bestowed only on the most distinguished scholars and artists. Then, to mark Shen's eightieth birthday in 1962, an exhibition of 120 of his works was held in Shanghai. Premier Zhou Enlai went to see them and Shen gave him a piece of his calligraphy that he had prepared specially for the occasion.

However, amid the widespread praise for Shen's calligraphy, some connoisseurs continued to voice doubts about his talent for the art. They argued that despite his undoubted skill in replicating the qualities of others, he had never managed to create a distinctive style of his own. Although there is an element of truth in this, Shen's work does at times have great power and beauty.

Since the 1950s Shen had been popular with his students because he had a great talent for explaining the art and techniques of calligraphy in simple language. He was an enthusiastic teacher: not only did he lecture frequently at the main cultural venues in Shanghai, he also used his own small house as a public classroom. In addition, he gave personal tuition to many young calligraphers who were later to become well known, among them Liu Zengfu (pp. 203–9).

Shen's eyesight had been deteriorating for some time, and by the mid-1960s it had become so bad that he could hardly see what he was doing. Nevertheless, he knew his art so well that he was able to continue writing even after he became virtually blind. Given this disability, Shen still managed to write remarkably well, but although his individual characters were often very good, the spacing between them was sometimes a little awkward and the lines tended to be crooked.

The Cultural Revolution

It was in this frail state that Shen watched with horror as the Cultural Revolution gathered momentum. Fearing a visit from the Red Guards, he took the precaution of destroying much of his work (both his own calligraphy and his writings on the subject), especially those pieces that were not either poems by Mao or in praise of Socialism. When the Red Guards did arrive at Shen's house they denounced him as a 'counter-revolutionary scholar' and compelled him to write out those characters as a banner, which they then pasted over the door of his house for all to see. He was harangued and humiliated, with little or no allowance made for the fact that he was over eighty years of age.

The Red Guards seized the few examples of Shen's calligraphy that they found in his house. Some of them, however, stole pieces for themselves – knowing enough to realize that the works had value, even if they did not personally appreciate them. Overnight, someone even snatched the 'counter-revolutionary scholar' banner from the front of Shen's house. Fortunately, he had been able to hide away the favourite small-scale pieces of calligraphy that had so long been on display in his home.

The harassment by the Red Guards did not last long. Following an enquiry from Premier Zhou Enlai about Shen's well-being, the local authorities began to protect him and his house. But even though his loving wife was able to remain with him, Shen's last years were not happy ones. When he died in 1971, at the age of eighty-eight, he was completely blind. His funeral was performed without ceremony and there were no obituaries to celebrate his achievements.

Eight years later, after Deng Xiaoping had assumed power, obituaries began to appear for many of the leading figures who had died during the Cultural Revolution. Shen Yinmo's were fulsome in their praise of his revolutionary character and the quality of his calligraphy, but of course no mention was made of the tender beauty of his love poetry.

What was not said at that time, but is said now, is that Shen's greatest achievement was the skill with which he used his talent and connections to keep the art of calligraphy alive in Shanghai during difficult times. For that, Shen deserves high praise.

YE GONGCHUO

1881–1968

The last of the great Qing innovators

When Ye Gongchuo was invited to return to China from Hong Kong in 1949, he was already nearly seventy years old and something of a legend. He had been a renowned reformer in the Republic of China and one of the few politicians of the Nationalist Party of Jiang Jieshi (Chiang Kaishek) to whom Mao took a liking. He was also one of China's top calligraphers.

A very cultured reformer

Ye was the talented scion of an old and distinguished mandarin family. By his twenties he had already become one of the top officials in the newly established Imperial Postal Bureau, later moving to the Railways Bureau. In the revolution of 1911 he sided with his fellow Cantonese reformer Sun Zhongshan (Sun Yatsen), who went on to become the first President of the Republic of China.

In the early years of the Republic, Ye made a name for himself as one of the most effective modernizers of the Chinese economy. He played a key role in developing China's banking system and railways, establishing the Communications University in Shanghai and sending people overseas to study railway engineering and bridge construction. He served at various times as Minister of Communications, Education and, briefly, Finance.

Unlike many other reformers, Ye had neither studied nor travelled overseas extensively in his youth. He did, however, go to Europe in 1918 to study the post-war reconstruction. In 1922 a political crisis in Beijing forced him to seek sanctuary in Japan, where he was greatly impressed by the pace of industrial development.

By the time he first withdrew from politics at the end of 1925, Ye had gained a reputation for honesty – a rarity among Nationalist leaders. At the same time his business activities were highly successful, which enabled him to become one of the great patrons of the arts in China. He even used his own money to protect a group of Northern Wei Buddhist statues that had been discovered by chance in Shanxi province. Himself a devout Buddhist, Ye was profoundly knowledgeable about Buddhist art.

He built up one of the best private art collections in China, having bought many pieces himself in the antique markets. Besides being a collector, Ye was a great believer in the value of museums and exhibitions. He was very

62 Ye Gongchuo was one of the last innovative calligraphers of the Qing dynasty.

proud of having organized the first art exhibition in China in 1928, and of having played a key role in arranging the famous 1936 exhibition of Chinese art at the Royal Academy in London. After his return to China in 1949, he made an even bigger gesture by giving many of his most valuable pieces to Chinese museums.

In addition, Ye was a patron of scholarship. He paid for the publication of works by many scholars in his native province of Guangdong. One of the projects he sponsored was *The Complete Lyrics of the Qing Dynasty*, which ran to many volumes and kept several professors busy for years. Ye himself was also a talented poet.

Although Ye was a committed and outward-looking reformer in national matters, his attitude towards family affairs was more traditional. He was willing to provide the finance for a female relative to study in the United States, but he expected his daughters to marry only into families of his own high social status.

Ye summed himself up well on a seal that he carved for himself, which read: 'If you can indulge yourself you can enjoy the entertainment, but you must not forget your goal' (*wan wu er bu sang zhi*). Huang Miaozi and Qi Gong, both of whom knew Ye Gongchuo well in Beijing during the 1950s and 1960s, found that he combined a certain strictness and self-discipline with a good sense of humour. In one respect Ye was like a little bird: bright-eyed, intense and high-spirited. Unlike little birds, however, he had a modest appetite. Even at banquets he would eat no more than a few vegetables.

Admired by Mao

While working as a librarian at Beijing University in the early 1920s, Mao Zedong began to take an interest in Ye, who by then was already well known as a great administrator and modernizer. But Mao soon came to realize that he was also a remarkably cultured man – which no doubt made him all the more interesting, as Mao had similar aspirations of his own. Above all, Mao sensed that Ye was a true patriot.

Ye served as Minister of Railways in 1932, but became increasingly disenchanted with the corruption of the Nationalists and their unwillingness to undertake far-reaching reforms. For a second time, he withdrew from politics. Mao knew of Ye's stance from several sources, including Zhang Shizhao (1881–1973), another Nationalist reformer who had links with the Communists.

After the outbreak of the Sino-Japanese War in 1937, Ye moved to Hong Kong. He had no wish to remain involved with the Nationalists, who had already been embroiled in conflict with the Communists for several years. Shortly after the Japanese had seized Hong Kong in 1941, they brought Ye back to Shanghai, where they hoped he would adopt a friendly attitude towards them, given that he had earlier sought refuge in Japan. But Ye was unwilling to do their bidding. At the end of the war he returned once more to Hong Kong. There he published books that he had written in recent years on the Buddhist scriptures, Chinese poetry and calligraphy.

Following the Communist victory in 1949, with Mao's approval Zhang Shizhao invited Ye to return to China. When Mao finally met Ye, soon after his return, he took an immediate liking to this slight, diminutive, soft-spoken man with his keen intelligence and his deep knowledge of Chinese culture.

Mao was particularly pleased by Ye's return because he saw it as a slap in the face for the Nationalists. At the same time he hoped that Ye's decision would encourage intellectuals and other influential 'patriotic' Chinese to support his own new regime. Ye, for his part, hoped that after more than a decade out of politics he would now be given an important post worthy of his talents.

Ye was quickly provided with a comfortable courtyarded house in the eastern part of the city. As much as Mao liked Ye, however, he wanted him to be a companion and a quiet figurehead, not a policy-maker. Reluctantly, Ye had to reconcile himself to being given jobs that were little more than sinecures: the directorship of the Academy of Traditional Chinese Painting and the vice-presidency, under Mao's cousin, of the newly created Historical and Cultural Research Institute – a place where retired top officials and academics could write their memoirs or simply while away their time. Sadly, the Party lacked the imagination to appoint Ye as head of the Palace Museum, a post for which he was eminently suited.

In other respects, Ye was well looked after. From time to time Mao would invite him to his home in the Zhongnanhai, particularly for his private birthday parties. He liked to talk to Ye about poetry and art, but not about politics. In his study Ye displayed one of the letters he had received from Mao. Since Mao was very particular about the recipients of his letters, this was widely, and correctly, interpreted as a sign of the special regard in which Mao held him.

As head of the Academy of Traditional Chinese Painting, Ye was naturally concerned about the welfare of artists. In 1956, during the early part of the 'Hundred Flowers Movement', he and Qi Gong (who was widely known as a scholar and painter) attended a meeting at Rong Bao Zhai, the main art shop and gallery in Beijing, where they called for a rise in artists'

Details of fig. 63

pay. A few months later, this seemingly innocuous demand resulted in both men being condemned as 'Rightists'.

Ye was convinced that his relationship with Mao was now over. As Mao's next birthday (26 December 1957) approached, he was therefore surprised to receive the usual invitation to his private party. Ye went along in trepidation, fearing arrest, But Mao was his usual cheerful and friendly self. He continued to relate to Ye as if he had never been branded a 'Rightist', and before too long Ye became one of the few people lucky enough to have this epithet lifted. When Mao celebrated his seventieth birthday in 1963, his only guests were four old non-Communists and some of their relatives. Those invited included both Ye and Zhang Shizhao.

Lacking a fulfilling role and disliking the growing hostility of the Communist Party towards intellectuals, Ye became disillusioned with the New China and consoled himself by devoting more and more of his time to scholarship and calligraphy.

Giving an air of greatness to small characters

Towards the end of the 1930s Ye was seen as one of the trinity of leading calligraphers in China, along with Yu Youren (who fled to Taiwan in 1949) and Shen Yinmo (pp. 67–73). These three men knew each other well and admired each other's work. Ye's mandarin upbringing had not been the ideal starting point from which to become a creative calligrapher, as the calligraphy of top mandarins had become very stylized and conformist. However, this did not hold him back. He had an exceptional determination not to be bound by mandarin conventions in matters of calligraphy, and during this period he gradually began to create a distinctive style of his own. As Qi Gong put it, Ye was able 'to give small-character calligraphy an air of greatness'.

As was customary in well-educated families, Ye had started studying calligraphy young, at around the age of five. As he developed he began to absorb characteristics of the styles of three famous calligraphers. He liked the way in which Yan Zhenqing (709–785) was forceful in his use of the brush, yet still able to compose characters tightly. And he admired the ability of Zhao Mengfu (1254–1322) to make each stroke full and rich, although he disliked the overall gracefulness of Zhao's style, which was too 'pretty' for his taste. He was also drawn to the skill of Chu Suiliang (596–658), who succeeded in creating variety in compositions that were tightly composed.

In essence, Ye believed that the key to good calligraphy was the composition of individual characters – an art that could best be mastered by

77

studying the seal and clerical scripts used on stone carvings during the Han (206 BC–AD 220) and Northern Wei (386–535) dynasties, along with the bamboo strips with writing on them that had been found in tombs dating from the Han period. He insisted that it was essential to study the stone carvings themselves, because the rubbings produced from them made the carvings look too soft.

Although Ye was in no doubt about the guidelines that calligraphers should follow, he rejected the idea of imposing strict rules. The composition of each character had, as it were, to be decided on the spot, according to the number of strokes involved and whether the character as a whole was long, short, wide or narrow. The composition was also affected by the size of the paper and how the characters could be arranged on it. From his own study and experience, Ye concluded that students should start by practising big characters, which he believed was the only way they could understand the full force of the brush.

In Ye's view, good calligraphy flowed naturally from a calm spirit and coordination between the brush and the whole of one's body. There was no question of writing with one's elbow on the table. The secret of success was to keep the wrist flexible, hold the brush tightly with one's fingers and make sure that the palm, wrist and elbow formed a straight line to the centre of the character. Only through such good posture and positioning was it possible to give force to the various strokes of the character – not only those going to the left or right, but those drawn vertically as well.

Ye practised what he preached and demonstrated great skill in writing characters both small and large. His energy tended to be reflected in the great speed at which he wrote, which often resulted in the appearance of strong diagonal strokes in his work. Even more often, his calligraphy was characterized by what might be described as a 'personal charm' (*yunwei*) that came from his skill in introducing subtle but constant changes of rhythm into the piece he was writing.

Characters imbued with personal charm

Ye was frequently obliged to produce calligraphy for his fellow members of the Historical and Cultural Research Institute, government or party officials and others. These pieces were usually based on innocuous phrases from the works of classical poets such as Li Bai (701–762), but as special gifts he often composed poems of his own, which tended to reflect his love of nature (fig. 63).

A fine example of Ye's intimate style of calligraphy was a gift he made, probably in the 1950s or early 1960s, for a friend he referred to as 'Master

63 This poem by Ye evokes the calm country atmosphere so much enjoyed by traditional Chinese scholars, especially those wishing to escape from the pressures of politics and city life.

Shiqing'. On the scroll he wrote out a poem he had written himself about a man walking home through the countryside in spring. It reads:

> *Here and there around the mountain, one hears farmers singing;*
> *A soft drizzle moistens my straw cape;*
> *The spring hills have a carefree air about them; and*
> *White cranes return, flying high over the mist that covers the top*
>   *of the woods.*
> *Over on the other side, the villages along the ravine are idle and quiet;*
> *Around the houses the thorn bushes have been cleared to make way*
>   *for flowers and grass;*
> *The buzzards and rooks have no fixed abode*
> *And return just as the bright clouds drift clear of the crags.*

Ye was clearly relaxed at the time he wrote this piece. The calligraphy contains those elements for which he was most renowned: structure, energy and personal charm.

Fear and honour

As the horror of the Cultural Revolution began to unfold in late 1966 and early 1967, Ye became deeply apprehensive. Mao assured him that he had nothing to fear, but he did not tell Ye that he had put him on a list of people who were to be protected from the Red Guards, nor that other eminent names on it were those of Madam Song Qingling, the widow of Sun Yatsen; Guo Moruo, the president of the Academy of Sciences; and Liu Yazi, who, like Ye, was a former Nationalist Party official with whom Mao had been exchanging poetry for years.

Although Ye sensed that he was under protection, he wondered how long it would last when he saw so many of his friends suffering terribly. In 1968 the publication in the *People's Daily* of an article accusing him of being the founder of 'bureaucratic capitalism' confirmed his worst fears. He collapsed with shock and was taken to hospital. On hearing of Ye's condition, Mao immediately sent him 2000 yuan, a sum equivalent to a top professor's salary for six months or that of a worker for nearly a decade. But the gift came too late. Ye was already unconscious and died a few days later.

Before the Cultural Revolution, Ye had written to Madam Song Qingling, who was then deputy chairman of the National People's Congress, telling her that because of his close links with her late husband he wished to be buried near Sun's mausoleum overlooking Nanjing, the first capital of the Republic. Madam Song therefore consulted Mao about the matter. Although Ye did not know it before he died, Mao granted his wish.

GUO MORUO

1892–1978

New China's 'Calligrapher Laureate'

Guo Moruo had much of the spirit of a 'renaissance man'. His life was marked by extraordinary intellectual energy and political agility. It is therefore hardly surprising that he excelled at calligraphy – an art he regarded as a defining characteristic of Chinese culture. In his later years Guo demonstrated not only a talent for survival, but also one for protecting the country's heritage during troubled times. Perhaps this is why there are many more examples of his calligraphy to be seen in public places in China today than there are of Mao Zedong's.

A love-hate relationship with Japan

Guo was born into a well-to-do merchant-landlord family that lived not far from the huge Buddha carved into the cliff above the river at Leshan in Sichuan province. From an early age he showed great talent with a brush and wrote big characters without resting his arm on the table. Later, however, he developed wide-ranging interests and became unwilling to devote a lot of time to the art. Instead of trying to learn the styles of several masters, as serious calligraphers often did, he chose to focus on one, Yan Zhenqing (709–785), who was renowned for the calm stability of his script.

In 1914, at the age of twenty-three, Guo went to Japan, which then was what today might be called a 'regional centre for European studies'. Spending his next nine years there, Guo studied Western medicine and began translating works of literature and philosophy ranging from Goethe to Galsworthy and from Nietzsche to Marx. He soon became well known as a liberal writer and poet, as well as a scholar of Chinese culture.

By the time Guo returned to China in 1923, he had become highly nationalistic and Marxist in his outlook. Three years later he enlisted at the Nationalist Party's military academy in Guangzhou (Canton), which was where he first met Zhou Enlai. The two men became lifelong friends. With the rupture between the Nationalists and the Communists in 1927, Zhou feared that leading Marxist intellectuals such as Guo would be assassinated. He therefore arranged for Guo and a number of others to return to Japan until the threat receded.

Over the next decade in Japan, Guo devoted much of his time to studying the history of ancient Chinese society, which he interpreted from a Marxist

64 Guo Moruo was often particularly pleased by his own skills as a calligrapher.

point of view. His attraction to Marxism was, however, counterbalanced by his passion for calligraphy. It was during this, his second stay in Japan that Guo embarked on his lifelong study of the evolution of calligraphy.

Guo had an unrivalled understanding of how the shape of characters had evolved, from the earliest, which were etched, to those created following the introduction of first the brush and then paper. This was one of the reasons why Guo took such an interest in Wang Xizhi (303–361), the first great artist of the brush. Wang's most admired work is a delightful essay known as *The Orchid Pavilion Preface*, in which he describes the power of literature to overcome the limitations of time. Guo could write this piece of calligraphy from memory, correct in every detail.

After the Sino-Japanese War had begun in 1937, Guo returned home to China once again. Before long he settled in the wartime capital, Chongqing, where he quickly assumed the mantle of China's leading left-wing writer and scholar. As a tribute to his success as a propagandist against Japan, his friends presented him with a giant calligraphy 'brush', which was more than two metres tall, so that he could write even bigger posters.

In Chongqing Guo again came into contact with Zhou Enlai, who was then heading the Communist Party's liaison mission to the Nationalist Government of Jiang Jieshi (Chiang Kaishek), with which there was a certain degree of cooperation in resisting the invading Japanese. Guo and Zhou saw a great deal of each other during these years.

Leader of the arts and sciences

When the Communists came to power in 1949, Guo was the obvious choice to be the president of the Academy of Sciences and to head the newly created Literature and Arts Federation. He devoted much effort to establishing the Academy as a centre of scholarship, while at the same time actively promoting the Party's policies in the arts and sciences. His power, however, was not his own but was derived from his patron, Zhou Enlai, one of the top people in the Communist Party.

During the early years of the New China, Guo, like many others, greatly admired Mao Zedong. But before long he began to realize that their political philosophies were very different. He welcomed Mao's invitation to the people in 1956 to say what they thought about the Party's role in developing a New China (the so-called 'Hundred Flowers Movement'). In the heady atmosphere of this period, the satirical magazine *Manhua* (*Cartoon*) carried a cheeky little ditty about Guo under the title 'Poets who run around for peace'. Within months, however, there was a torrent of criticism of the new regime. Feeling that the situation was getting out of control, the Party responded in a draconian manner. Most of those who had spoken out, especially the intellectuals, were quickly criticized, silenced and punished. Some people were sent to labour camps before joining those who had been relegated to the fringes of society, where they were to remain for the next twenty years.

Once an individual had been attacked by the Party, Guo believed that he or she was, to all intents and purposes, a 'lost soul'. In order to protect his own position and that of others, he therefore collaborated in condemning protesters. Although within his cherished Academy Guo quietly protected many scholars, those of his friends and colleagues who suffered during this period never forgave him for behaving as he did.

The events of the late 1950s left Guo feeling vulnerable. He knew that Premier Zhou Enlai and Foreign Minister Chen Yi did not share Mao's hostility towards intellectuals, but there were many powerful figures in the Party who did, and who mistrusted Guo on account of his elitist interests. Guo's fears for his own safety led him to produce calligraphy in support of political campaigns. For example, following Mao's launch of the 'Great Leap Forward' and the creation of the People's Communes in 1958, he composed this couplet, which he wrote out with a brush:

The People's Communes are great in every way.
The Party's General Line gets brighter every day.

Pieces of his calligraphy such as this were reproduced by the highly skilled woodcarvers at Rong Bao Zhai and then widely sold.

Despite the political strains under which he worked, Guo continued to develop his own style of calligraphy. By the mid-1950s it had become freer, with a richness of brushwork that was decidedly his own. He used the tip of the brush to good effect, excelling in a technique that one might call 'counter-movement', whereby the start of the brushstroke is concealed by beginning it in one direction, then quickly turning the tip of the brush in the opposite direction onto its right course.

In considering Guo's calligraphy, one has to bear in mind that he was an astute political survivor with complex emotions. Although he could be cheerful and at times playful in dealing with acquaintances and contacts, there seems to have been no great warmth in his personal relationships, even within his family. Indeed, when under political pressure Guo could be almost icy towards his children. It is possible to detect in his calligraphy traces of those moments when he was feeling relaxed and open towards his wife and children, but even under pressure he was such a master of technique that he could still produce fine calligraphy.

Detail of fig. 67

Because Guo was regarded as the leading cultural figure in China, his brush was much in demand. He created the name plaques for the Palace Museum, the Summer Palace and Beihai Park in Beijing, as well as those for historic monuments in many other cities and scenic spots. He also provided the calligraphy to embellish the logo of the Bank of China, as well as producing work for several hotels, restaurants and shops (including Rong Bao Zhai and his favourite ancient coin shop in Liulichang Street). Before the Cultural Revolution there was far more of Guo's calligraphy on display in Beijing and elsewhere than there was of Mao's. Needless to say, this did not escape Mao's notice.

Guo often gave pieces of his calligraphy to prominent people in the hope that it would help him win their favour. In these pieces he often combined his artistic skill with an ability to write truly classical Chinese verse. This was a rare talent, even among his gifted contemporaries. He also had a flair for reworking the poetry of others into new forms. As gifts for those old revolutionaries who had been on the Long March or fought against the Japanese or Jiang Jieshi, he could always find an apt quote from Mao. Sometimes he would record his impressions of places they knew, so that his poem would be linked to events that were etched into their memories. For fellow scholars and artists he would produce elegant, erudite works that usually discreetly flattered the recipient.

Flattery was much in evidence in the piece Guo presented in 1964 to his friend Marshal Chen Yi (pp. 91–9), who had been Foreign Minister since 1958. At that time China was at odds not only with the Soviet Union, over the strategy of the international Communist movement, but also with the United States, which was concerned in particular that China might stir up revolution in the Third World. Guo chose to write out for Chen Yi a pair of massive scrolls, more than 3.5 metres long. Both panels were embellished with characters from one of Guo's most graphic poems – the same one that later inspired Mao to write one of his own most famous poems, known as *Manjianghong*. In his poem Guo declared that China would succeed in:

> *Shoring up the falling heavens*
> *and creating order from the reign of chaos.*

By giving Chen Yi this couplet, Guo was implying that his friend was playing just such a role in the political developments of the day.

Guo's concern about his political vulnerability was compounded in the early 1960s, when he began to sense that Mao was reacting increasingly like a threatened emperor rather than a confident leader. As early as 1964, two years before the Cultural Revolution, Guo sought to protect his position

83

by declaring publicly that all his previous writings were 'strictly speaking, worthless'.

Anticipating worse times to come, Guo made a special effort to cultivate his links with Mao. He was pleased that the poems he had written and sent to him in 1961 and 1963 had served as the catalyst for two of Mao's own works. In both cases Mao had specifically credited Guo by heading the poem 'Reply to Comrade Guo Moruo'. The second poem, widely known as *Manjianghong*, the name of the tune to which it is recited, became one of Mao's most popular works. It was written to strengthen the resolve of his colleagues during China's continuing disputes with the Soviet Union. In it Mao compares China's critics to flies, ants and mayflies, while China itself is presented as an irresistible force. His stirring poem contains the lines:

So many deeds cry out to be done...
Time presses.
Seize the day, seize the hour!

In 1964 Guo was the first person to produce a book of calligraphy containing all thirty-four of Mao's published poems. Many connoisseurs rate this as one of his finest calligraphic achievements. Guo's brushwork, however, was lyrical. He made no attempt to match Mao's own wild cursive script. Privately, Guo wrote out Mao's poem *Manjianghong* as a fine, dramatic piece of cursive script for his own pleasure and that of his family. It was as if he wanted to demonstrate that Mao was not the only person capable of working in this style (fig. 65).

Many Chinese believed that Guo had close personal links with Mao, but Guo himself recognized that their relationship did not really amount to much. The few occasions on which they had met were formal ones. Moreover, the much-admired piece of Mao's calligraphy that Guo proudly displayed in his study had actually been obtained under false pretences. Guo had conveyed to Mao a request from the leaders of Jingangshan (a revolutionary base in 1928) for him to produce an inscription for them. Mao complied and sent the piece to Guo, assuming that he would forward it to the revolutionaries in Jingangshan. But such was Guo's passion for having a piece of Mao's own work that he sent them a photograph of the scroll and kept the original for himself.

Among Guo's best pieces are reflections on a visit to the Temple of Confucius at Qufu, the city where Confucius was born; anecdotes about how much he laughed at a comedian's imitation of snoring; recollections of a cruise down the Yangzi River to the Three Gorges; a description of a walk in the countryside; advice to his son on how to achieve flexibility in his

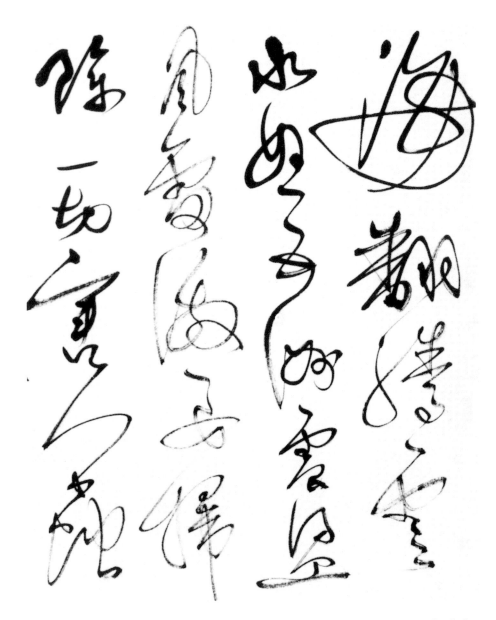

calligraphy; and a poem to his wife, written on her birthday, in which he praises her calligraphic achievements with the uncritical acclaim expected of a spouse. Privately, he also wrote out one of Mao's poems in which Mao refers with exquisite delicacy to the loss of his first wife.

One of Guo's livelier pieces resulted from a visit he paid in the summer of 1962 to the Wu Yi mountains in Fujian province (fig. 66). He was exhilarated by this beauty spot, which is famous for its strange outcrops of rock that look like tall stone drums:

From the thick pine forest over the pass,
I can look down and see the whole Mingjiang valley
in a single glance.

Some men come here to play the stone drums,
but I just wish to stretch out
and touch the heavenly blue above.

85

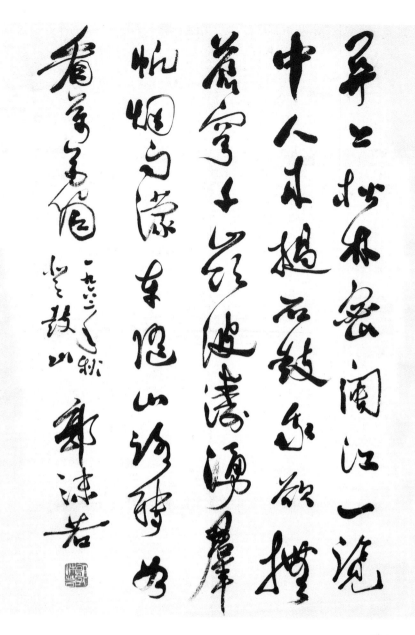

66 Guo's visit to the Wu Yi mountains in 1962 inspired him to produce calligraphy at its most relaxed.

67 Guo was always thrilled by famous cultural sites. His visit to the Pu Zhao Temple on Mount Taishan, the huge ancient pine reputed to be more than 1,500 years old, inspired him to write these elegant verses:

As this pine has flourished since the
Six Dynasties,
it should be ranked as a Minister of
the First Class.

Some of its branches lunge down
like a dragon craving for the earth,
while others rise like a fiery phoenix
to the sky.

The calligraphy is wonderful, Guo's dark, dry brushwork reminding the beholder of the bark and needles of that ancient pine. Feeling obliged, however, to balance his eloquence with a reference to China's needs, Guo added:

May such a blessing be transformed
into sweet rain
that will give China bumper harvests
for thousands of years.

I see a thousand hills billowing like waves
with boats sailing through the misty rain.

And as my car runs along this mountain route
the scenery keeps changing with kaleidoscopic wonder.

In this piece Guo's calligraphy has an unusually jaunty air about it, his brush often lightly linking one character to another (see also fig. 67).

The Cultural Revolution

Guo was horrified when Mao unleashed the Cultural Revolution in the summer of 1966, even though troops were soon sent to protect his house. His son, who was serving in the army, was so frightened about what might happen to him on account of his father's position and interests that he committed suicide in 1967. His death disturbed Guo deeply.

What Guo did not know was that at the beginning of the Cultural Revolution Mao had approved a list of prominent people who should be protected. The first person on the list was Madam Song Qingling, the widow of China's first president, Sun Zhongshan (Sun Yatsen), who at that time was vice-chairman of the Standing Committee of the National People's Congress. Guo's name was second on the list, followed by those of a number of non-Communists, such as Ye Gongchuo and Liu Yazi, who had won Mao's favour years earlier and had remained out of politics.

During the first three years of the Cultural Revolution, Guo made few public appearances. From his home, he kept in touch with Premier Zhou Enlai by letter and occasionally by telephone. But by 1969 it was clear to him that Mao was beginning to worry about the damage his Cultural Revolution was causing to China's international reputation.

Having sensed this concern, Guo made a bold and astute move. He wrote to Zhou Enlai suggesting that, given the important archaeological discoveries that had been made by workers and peasants since the beginning of the Cultural Revolution, there would be merit in resuming the publication of China's three leading archaeological journals. Guo knew that this proposal would have the wholehearted support of Kang Sheng, head of the secret police. It was, after all, Kang Sheng's calligraphy that had embellished the masthead of the journal of the Institute of Archaeology since the 1950s. When the three journals reappeared in 1970, they were the first scholarly publications to have been seen in China since the start of the Cultural Revolution.

As his next step, Guo promoted the idea of staging an 'Exhibition of Cultural Relics excavated during the Great Proletarian Cultural Revolution'.

He arranged for a stunning collection of objects to be displayed in the reopened Forbidden City in 1972. Guo made the exhibition politically acceptable by portraying these items as important evidence of the skill and culture of the workers who had made them, rather than as symbols of the old ruling class who had commissioned them.

Archaeology also provided Guo with a pretext for publishing a book praising China's two best-known Tang dynasty poets, Li Bai and Du Fu. He prepared the text in 1969, when the border dispute with the USSR was still a heated issue. Guo gave his work a suitable degree of 'political correctness' by arguing in his preface that recent archaeological evidence had proved that although the place where Li Bai had been born was at that time a part of western China, the area had since been seized by Russia and was now controlled by the Soviet Union. Mao liked the book for this reason, but possibly even more so because Guo's views on poetry had grown closer to his own. Back in the 1950s Guo had favoured Du Fu's astute insights into human feelings and behaviour over the more romantic outlook of Li Bai. In his new book, however, he had reversed his position. Published in 1972, Guo's book was the first scholarly work of literature to have appeared since the launch of the Cultural Revolution nearly seven years earlier.

Developments in China's foreign policy soon gave Guo a welcome opportunity both to protect his own position and to help other scholars. When the political situation stabilized in the early 1970s, Mao wanted more foreign dignitaries to visit China as part of the campaign to enlist support for China in its border dispute with the Soviet Union and against the continued international recognition of Taiwan. But preparations for the arrival of such visitors raised the awkward question of who should play host to them.

As a result of the recent political upheavals in China, there was hardly anyone of suitable rank available to receive many of the foreign dignitaries. After Mao and Zhou Enlai, the next in line was Guo, who, besides being president of the Academy of Sciences, was also vice-chairman of the Standing Committee of the National People's Congress (which was then very much a rubber-stamp parliament). Guo skilfully exploited diplomatic visits of this kind to secure the release of prominent scholars, on the grounds that 'experts' were needed to take part in high-level discussions. In his diplomatic role he found himself improbably having to take an interest in table tennis as China became involved in the so-called 'ping-pong diplomacy' that preceded and followed the world championships in Tokyo in 1971, culminating in President Nixon's visit to China the following year. It was in this context that I first met Guo.

68 Guo's popular poem *Smash the Gang of Four to Smithereens* was published in the *People's Daily* to celebrate their downfall.

水調歌頭 粉碎四人帮

大快人心事，揭出四人帮。政治流氓文痞，狗头军师张。还有精生白骨，自比一枝红杏，蓬壑寺。篡党夺权者，一枕黄梁。

野心大，阴谋毒，诡计狂。真是罪恶滔天，迫害红太阳！权者一枕黄粱。

Guo's deep knowledge of Japanese culture and language ensured that he was also closely involved in the development of Sino-Japanese relations during this period. Since 1949 he had revisited Japan on several occasions and received many Japanese visitors to China. Perhaps not surprisingly, calligraphy played an important part in these exchanges, for it was an art form shared by both countries. Following the re-establishment of diplomatic relations between China and Japan in 1972, Guo was quick to suggest to Premier Zhou Enlai, and through him to Chairman Mao, that the occasion be celebrated by the publication in *People's China* of works by each country's contemporary calligraphers, followed up by exhibitions in Tokyo and Beijing. These public celebrations allowed calligraphers who had been relegated to obscurity, such as Lin Sanzhi, to come into the limelight.

Despite these diplomatic successes – indeed, because of some of them – Guo fell out of favour with Jiang Qing and the other members of the Gang of Four. Jiang's dislike of Guo went back a long way. During the late 1960s, for example, he had declined her request to serve as cultural adviser to one of her 'revolutionary operas' on the grounds that he was too deaf. Jiang Qing had resented his refusal, and she had a long memory.

As Mao's health deteriorated, the Gang of Four launched a nationwide campaign to criticize Lin Biao and the great philosopher Confucius, an odd pairing of new 'enemies of the State' calculated to veil their true purpose. Guo could see exactly what was happening. He told his wife that their real target was Premier Zhou. Soon afterwards, the Gang of Four began to describe Zhou as 'the new Confucius' because of his patrician character and moderate outlook. Guo knew that if Zhou fell, he would too.

Guo also recognized that his own admiration for Confucius was his Achilles' heel. Although Mao had declared during the early years of the Cultural Revolution that Confucius had been a bad influence on China, Guo had never shared this view, nor had he voiced it. In not concurring, he had tacitly opposed Mao's views, so it is not surprising that this new anti-Confucian campaign sent shivers down his spine. In 1974 Jiang Qing stepped up the pressure by asking Guo to write an article attacking the semi-legendary Duke of Zhou, whom Confucius had regarded as a model ruler. He never replied and soon became very ill.

Zhou Enlai died on 8 January 1976. Guo was deeply upset by his death. On the day it was announced, he wrote in his diary: 'A hero has left, never to return.' Two weeks later he wrote a poem about Zhou Enlai that was probably the deepest expression of feeling which this otherwise emotionally detached man had ever made. In it he declared that Zhou's death was like a giant star falling from the sky. He ended by quoting Laozi: 'Neither the vastness of the heavens, nor all the expanse of the earth is big enough to bury your greatness.' On 21 October 1976, ten days after the arrest of the Gang of Four, Guo rose from his sickbed and with a trembling hand took up his brush. The poem he wrote, for publication in the *People's Daily*, was entitled *Smash the Gang of Four to Smithereens* (fig. 68).

In translation, Guo's words sound wooden and contrived. Nevertheless, they were extremely popular at the time. Not only did they express the public mood, but they have a rhythm and catchiness that is tied to the metre of a popular Chinese poem. The piece reflected Guo's hope that the downfall of the Gang of Four would usher in a new era.

In the spring of 1977, when he was feeling a little better, Guo wrote one of his last important pieces of calligraphy. It was a couplet placed under the horizontal title *Songs of Triumph to be Loudly Sung*:

> *With the smashing of the Gang of Four, spring returns to China.*
> *Now there is all the vitality needed to modernize the country.*

That autumn Guo made his final public appearance at the opening of the National Conference of Science and Technology, at which he spoke on the importance of modernizing China. On 12 June 1978, he died.

After his funeral, Deng Xiaoping sang Guo's praises. He commended him for the part he had played in helping to modernize China, for his work in promoting Chinese culture, and for his talent as a calligrapher. To this day, however, many of the people who in the past had suffered and not received any help from Guo, for whatever reason, are still highly critical of him.

Perhaps, as time passes, Guo's political achievements may come to be seen in a slightly different light. It is interesting to note that before the Cultural Revolution it was difficult for him to protect others because of his very public position, but during it, when he was protected, he was able to work skilfully behind the scenes to make traditional culture acceptable once again, helping many of those scholars who had suffered. He played a key part in keeping the art of calligraphy alive during one of the darkest periods of China's history.

CHEN YI

1901–72

The poetic revolutionary

69 Chen Yi loved to write out his poems as pieces of calligraphy.

Marshal Chen Yi was a formidable military commander with both a passion and a flair for calligraphy. Many Chinese, and foreigners as well, regard him as the most likeable of the leaders of the Chinese revolution. Although there were others equally cultured, he was more genial and jovial than any of them. His willingness to champion moderation, and his enjoyment of the good life and friendship, won him great popularity.

From poet to revolutionary commander

Chen Yi was born in Sichuan province, where his father was a well-educated district magistrate. After the Republican revolution in 1911, the family fell on hard times. Chen Yi's father wanted his son to have a good education, but could only afford to send him to a vocational school. Fortunately, Chen Yi's great love of poetry and literature sustained his own determination to obtain a good education.

By 1919 Chen Yi had done sufficiently well in his studies to be selected to go to France on a work-study programme. Whilst there he developed a taste for the work of several French poets and writers. It soon became clear, however, that Chen Yi was not just interested in the arts. In 1922 he and a hundred of his fellow students were sent back to China following their involvement in political protests.

On his return to China, Chen Yi continued his studies at the recently opened Sino-French University in Beijing. At this stage he still wanted to be a poet, but as his anger at the misery and injustice he saw in China mounted, he became increasingly involved in political debate. After just one year in Beijing, he joined the Communist Party. Four years later, in 1927, he became one of the founding members of the People's Liberation Army. Over the next six years he spent much of his time with Mao Zedong, who was soon to emerge as the leader of the Chinese Communist Party. In 1934, when Mao's troops were forced to flee north to the Communist stronghold of Yanan, Chen Yi remained in central China.

During their first years together in the new Communist army, relations between Mao and Chen Yi were close. They both wrote poetry, though in different styles: Mao's was classical, while that of the better educated and more widely travelled Chen Yi was based on modern spoken Chinese, which was much easier for ordinary people to understand. When Mao felt at risk he would entrust copies of his poems to Chen Yi for safekeeping.

It was not until 1944, after a separation of ten years, that Mao and Chen Yi finally met up again in Yanan. By then, Chen Yi was one of Mao's most renowned military commanders. He liked to express himself through his poetry and felt that it was at its best when he had written it out in calligraphy. Much of Chen Yi's poetry, like Mao's, was about the political and military events in which he had been embroiled. But a greater number of his poems were personal, such as those he composed for his wife.

Shortly after he reached Yanan in 1944, Chen Yi settled down to write out all his poems in a simple album. He did so in small running-script characters, using a slightly hard, wet brush. He took delight in using the lightest of strokes and contrasting the general roundness of his script with firmer, elongated vertical strokes – a style which reflected that of Wang Xizhi, the great fourth-century calligrapher.

70 This is the first page of Chen Yi's poem *Mount Mogan*, inspired by a visit to that mountain in 1952. He wrote it out on the traditional red-lined official paper printed by the new 'Shanghai People's Government'. Later, he wrote other poems on both Foreign Ministry and State Council paper.

Patron of the arts

After the Japanese surrender in 1945, Chen Yi played a key role in wresting control of China's eastern seaboard from the forces of Jiang Jieshi (Chiang Kaishek). In 1949 he led the final rout in eastern China before marching unopposed into Shanghai, from where Jiang had just fled. In 1950 he was appointed Mayor of Shanghai.

Shanghai was still China's most cosmopolitan city, but it had changed greatly over the preceding decade as a result of Japanese occupation and the civil war in China. When the Communist forces reached the city, most remaining foreigners decided that the time had come for them to leave. Shanghai was in a terrible and chaotic state, swamped with refugees. To make matters worse, industry and commerce were at an all-time low. Not only had the foreign companies gone, but the majority of Shanghai's foremost businessmen had fled to Taiwan or Hong Kong, together with their key workers and much of their machinery.

Chen Yi's moderate views and faith in the future of Shanghai greatly aided his efforts to win people over to the new regime. He paid particular attention to the large number of scholars, writers and artists still living in the city. Many were given good jobs, and for those for whom there was nothing suitable in the 'New China' he set up a Cultural and Historical Bureau (a similar one later being set up in Beijing). This bureau, lodged in a fine old mansion, provided sinecures for poets, writers, calligraphers and artists. Its members were supposed to be over sixty, but Chen Yi ensured that judgements of eligibility were linked more closely to talent than to age.

92

The scholar who benefited most was Shen Yinmo (pp. 67–73), who was now living in Shanghai. As we have seen, Shen was widely revered for having been one of the leading members of the May Fourth Movement, which in 1919 gave impetus to reform in early Republican China. He was also one of China's leading scholar-calligraphers. Chen Yi gave Shen an important position in the Municipal Cultural Bureau, which was charged with implementing his three major cultural projects: the creation of a Museum of Chinese Antiquities, a Chinese municipal library and a Symphony Orchestra. Long after he left Shanghai, Chen Yi continued to send traditional gifts of money to Shen at Chinese New Year.

Chen Yi greatly enjoyed being mayor. He liked both the work and the 'perks'. He lived in a series of lovely old houses, the third and last of which was in Xinguo Road (and is now the Xinguo Guest House). Each of these residences provided a worthy setting for the many attractive items of furniture and works of art that he had collected. He would often invite friends who were poets or calligraphers to his home. Shen was a frequent guest and gave Chen Yi some fine examples of his work.

As well as being mayor, Chen Yi was commander of the Shanghai Military District, which took in several neighbouring provinces. His trips to the military district enabled him to indulge his interest in antiquities beyond the confines of Shanghai. Although his military duties took priority, it was well known that on such visits he always hoped there would still be time to visit local museums or cultural sites. Sometimes he wrote poems on the subject; in 1952, for example, he wrote one about a visit to Mount Mogan (fig. 70), which had been the most popular resort among foreigners living in Shanghai. The poem described the luxuriant vegetation, the beautiful effects created by the mist on the mountain, and the peace of the night. In the final verse Chen Yi added that the scenery was even better now that it 'belonged to the people' (a polite way of expressing his pleasure that the Communists had won the civil war and the foreigners had left).

Chen Yi's contentment with life in the mid-1950s brought a new liveliness to his brush. When he paid his first visit to the seaside resort of Qingdao in 1954, he composed a poem about the history of this port city (fig. 71), once a German colony and later a Japanese one, which he sent to Guo Moruo (pp. 80–90), the president of the Academy of Sciences.

A year later Chen Yi returned to Chengdu, which inspired him to write a poem about growing up in the city as a child. In it he makes an implicit contrast between the old and the new China. The last four lines play on the idea that the spring flowers are now finished, but Chengdu is already 'blossoming' under the rule of the Communist Party (fig. 72).

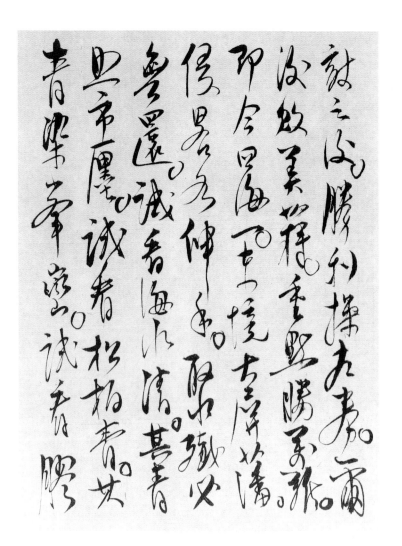

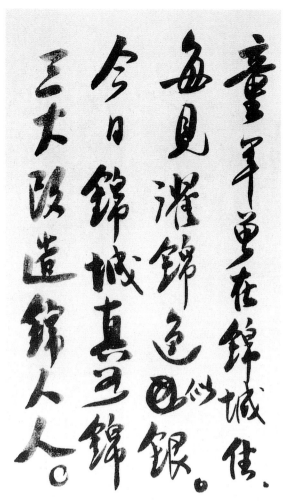

These two pieces display very different styles of brushwork. The lightness of the brushstrokes in *Qingdao* conjures up sea breezes and the bright freshness of white-capped waves, suggesting that Chen Yi was very relaxed when he wrote out his poem as a piece of calligraphy. In *Chengdu*, on the other hand, he used not only a softer and thicker brush than usual, but also a much moister ink, thereby creating subtle variations of tone.

Chen Yi's contentment was also evident in the relaxed style of the calligraphic titles he created to go above the entrances of the new Shanghai Municipal Museum and Library. Like Mao, Chen Yi had never mastered the technique of writing large characters, so his fairly small script had to be enlarged for the purpose. (Although both the museum and the library moved to new locations in the 1990s, each continued to use Chen Yi's name plaque.)

He then started to write harmonious larger characters with thicker strokes, in the style of Su Dongpo (1037–1101), one of his favourite poets. He used this style on the memorial near Shanghai that he had erected to honour the writer Xia Yongyi (d. 1646) and his son Xia Wanchun, known as a child prodigy for his poetry, who had died resisting the Manchu

71 Part of Chen Yi's poem *Qingdao* (left)

72 Part of Chen Yi's poem *Chengdu*

invasion of China. This was Chen Yi's way of paying homage to two men he regarded as both literary and nationalist heroes.

The best-known example of Chen Yi's use of thicker brushstrokes is to be seen in his title calligraphy for a book which the Shanghai Municipal Museum published in 1959 on its painting collection. It was one of the finest pieces of colour printing produced anywhere at that time, in which the reproductions of the paintings were enhanced by being printed on silk or paper according to the original medium used. The book was bound in dark blue velvet and protected by a rich silk-covered box. Chen Yi's calligraphy adorned both the cover and the title page. His pride in the work is reflected in his brushstrokes.

Growing differences with Mao

During the mid-1950s Chen Yi received a number of promotions. In 1954, while retaining his post as mayor, he was appointed as one of the vice-premiers; his responsibilities were to include culture and science. The following year he was one of several top-ranking officers promoted to the newly created rank of Marshal, and in 1956 he was elected to the Politburo of the Communist Party. It was not until he became Foreign Minister in 1958 that he was finally replaced as mayor of Shanghai.

As much as Chen Yi liked dealing with cultural and scientific matters, this role highlighted his differences with Mao over the importance of intellectuals in the development of China. Chen Yi felt that they had a crucial role to play in modernizing China and, as he had shown in Shanghai, that they could be won over to the Socialist cause through gentle persuasion. He disagreed with Mao's campaigns against the intelligentsia and resented his distrust of them. Nevertheless, out of respect for Mao he kept fairly quiet when tens of thousands of intellectuals were branded as 'Rightists' in 1957–8.

As Foreign Minister, Chen Yi worked closely with Premier Zhou Enlai on a number of difficult national problems. At this time the main issue was China's relations with the Soviet Union, which were going from bad to worse – a process made all the more nerve-racking by Khrushchev's erratic temperament. At the height of the dispute, in 1961, Guo Moruo presented Chen Yi with a pair of huge scrolls of calligraphy. They bore an apt quote from one of Guo's own poems (written in response to one by Mao), which featured a stirring couplet conveying a powerful image of fortitude and progress (see p. 83). This was a flattering gift, clearly implying that Guo regarded Chen Yi as playing a heroic part in China's confrontation with the Soviet Union.

That same year Chen Yi attended the Laos Peace Conference in Geneva, where, over the next year, he helped achieve an accord. With him at his place at the conference table Chen Yi always had his calligraphy brush and ink, and he could often be seen using them to annotate documents. During the boring parts of the conference (of which there were many) he would appear particularly engrossed in his brushwork. Quite possibly he was working on his poems.

One of Chen Yi's most beautiful calligraphic renderings of his own poems is the one he did of *Kunming* (fig. 73). He had spent New Year's Day 1961 in Kunming together with Premier Zhou Enlai, with whom he was travelling to Burma. After describing the delights of the celebrations in the city, he goes on to refer to their send-off at the airport and the flight to Burma, which suggests that he wrote the poem on the plane.

73 Chen Yi wrote out his poem *Kunming* on two sheets of finely decorated traditional paper.

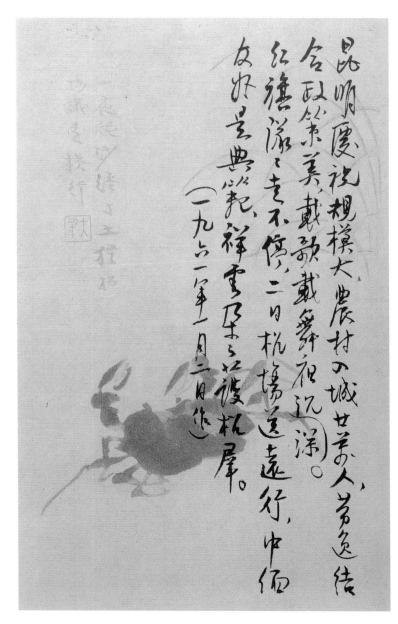
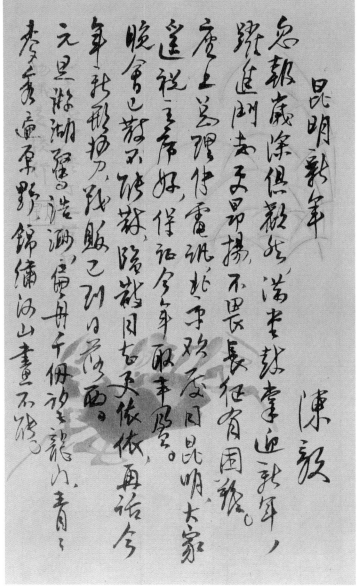

Rank upon rank of red flags in a never-ending march
See us off on our long journey from the airport.
A new leaf is written in the annals of the friendship between
    China and Burma.
Cloud upon auspicious cloud protects our fleet of planes.

In Rangoon, Chen Yi and his beautiful wife both wore traditional Burmese attire to one of the banquets to which they were invited – which meant that her blouse was transparent. It was undoubtedly the first time that the bra of a Chinese leader's wife had appeared on the political scene.

From Chen Yi's point of view, the Geneva conference was a less fraught affair than some of those he attended in China. The one that troubled him most was the high-level Party meeting in Guangzhou in 1962, when the question of the role of intellectuals came up again. Chen Yi argued that they should be treated better, even though he knew that Mao would not approve of his expressing this opinion. Neither did Mao's displeasure deter him in July 1966 from quietly beginning to voice his concerns about Mao's increasingly autocratic behaviour.

Victim of the Cultural Revolution

When Mao unleashed the Cultural Revolution on China in 1966, Chen Yi had a dark premonition of what was going to happen. Late that autumn, as the temperature fell sharply and the leaves turned red on the hills to the west of Beijing, he poured out his feelings in a poem entitled *The Red Leaves of the Western Hills*. The thrust of it was that in the end the true and decent revolutionaries were the ones who would prevail. As he put it in his opening lines:

The red leaves of the Western Hills are splendid,
    the colder it gets, the better their colour.
Revolutionaries are like this too,
    with struggle creating heroes.

From the outset Chen Yi objected to the Red Guards. In February 1967, just a month after being forced to undertake public self-criticism, Chen Yi and a number of other marshals and vice-premiers confronted Lin Biao, Mao's chosen successor, and Jiang Qing, Mao's wife, over the excesses of the Red Guards.

As the Cultural Revolution became increasingly violent in the summer of that year, Chen Yi warned Mao against the growing barbarism being advocated by Lin Biao and the Gang of Four. This was not what Mao wanted to hear. He responded by telling the Red Guards that Chen Yi was now one of those who could be criticized, although he should still not be harmed.

With considerable difficulty, Premier Zhou Enlai managed to extract Chen Yi from the increasing menace of the Red Guards and place him under what amounted to protective confinement within the leadership compound of Zhongnanhai. Mao ostracized Chen Yi, but still valued his opinions on major national issues, despite the fact that Chen Yi no longer had direct control over the foreign ministry. In 1969 Mao tasked Chen Yi and three other marshals to carry out 'research' on international relations with the support of experts from the ministry. Their subsequent report played down the risk of war with the United States. In a personal report Chen Yi argued that since the talks between American and Chinese diplomats in Warsaw had made no progress, perhaps the time had come for China and the United States to meet at ministerial or even higher level. His report helped pave the way for the secret talks with Dr Henry Kissinger.

The decline in Chen Yi's influence within the Party was underscored at the Ninth Party Congress that year, at which Mao and Lin Biao presented their radical agenda for the Cultural Revolution. Although Chen Yi was re-elected to the Central Committee, he was dropped from the Politburo. But Mao still respected him and needed his help. Chen Yi had retained his vice-chairmanship of the Central Military Affairs Commission, and when Mao feared a surprise attack on Beijing, he arranged for Chen Yi to be one of the leaders evacuated from the capital.

Relations between Mao and Chen Yi continued to worsen. At the Central Committee plenum held at Lushan the following year, in October 1970, Mao condemned Chen Yi as a 'sham Marxist' and an 'anti-Party careerist'. Nevertheless, later that month he was allowed to return to Beijing, largely because he was increasingly suffering from intestinal cancer.

Although Chen Yi still lived with his family and was not treated badly, as a gregarious individual he hated being under house arrest. In September 1971 he not only had the satisfaction of hearing that Lin Biao had been killed while trying to flee to the Soviet Union after his planned coup had been exposed, but he was asked to break the news to senior Party members. Meanwhile, however, his health was deteriorating dramatically.

Chen Yi spent his last months in hospital, comforted by his wife. When he died on 6 January 1972 it seemed that he would receive few honours until at the last minute, in a fit of remorse, Mao decided to attend the funeral. Belatedly, he acknowledged that Chen Yi had been loyal and had been right to question the professed loyalty of Lin Biao. At the funeral Mao told Chen Yi's widow, 'Chen Yi was a good comrade. He was a good man. He made a contribution to China's revolution and world revolution. He won great merit. This is the final conclusion.'

The publication of Chen Yi's poems and calligraphy

After Chen Yi's death, his wife, herself now suffering from cancer, struggled to put together a collection of her husband's poems. Although she had completed the task by the end of 1973, she was unable to publish her book because of the influence of Jiang Qing.

Even after the overthrow of the Gang of Four in October 1976, several more months passed before the book could be published. When it finally came out the following year, it was quickly bought up by the many people who had a great affection for Chen Yi. Two of his poems about the war, *Meiling San Zhang* ('Three Poems on Plum Ridge') and *Gan Nan Youji Ci* ('Song of the Southern Jiangxi Guerrillas'), had long been popular. But the book's success was further enhanced when word got around about the final poem that appeared in it, *The Red Leaves of the Western Hills*.

For many Chinese people *The Red Leaves* was deeply moving. It not only reflected their own suffering, but reminded them of all the friends they had lost in the madness of the Cultural Revolution. It also made them feel that, through their ability to survive, they had won a great moral victory and gained a new determination to enjoy life – a sentiment that would have delighted Chen Yi.

In response to the popularity of the book, Chen Haosu, one of Chen Yi's sons, published a facsimile edition of the calligraphic versions of the poems (including several drafts) that his father had written over the years. Some of the poems had been written out on traditional calligraphy paper, while others were on the official red-lined paper of bodies such as the Ministry of Foreign Affairs and the State Council (see fig. 70). It is not clear whether Chen Yi used this paper simply because it was readily to hand when he had a little spare time in which to write his calligraphy, or whether he was really bored at work. Whatever the answer, the book is a delightful insight into this engaging man's passion for both poetry and calligraphy.

On the ninetieth anniversary of Chen Yi's birth in 1991, Jiang Zemin, who was then mayor of Shanghai, delivered a speech in Beijing warmly praising him. This paved the way for the Shanghai Municipality to erect a large statue of Chen Yi on the Bund in 1996. Although there remain some statues of Mao which are bigger than that of Chen Yi, his can be seen as a truer reflection of the enormous affection inspired by the man it honours.

DENG SANMU

1898–1963

'In vain, I try to stir their senses'

When the Communists took over Shanghai in 1949, Deng Sanmu was not only one of China's most popular calligraphers, but also one of its most renowned eccentrics. Such an irascible character was doomed to run foul of the authorities. When this happened, in almost tragicomic circumstances, Deng responded with spirit. Once again, he began to sign his work 'Lord of the Shits'.

Deng had had a rather unusual education for the period. With an eye to the future, his father had sent him to an English secondary school in Shanghai, at which, of course, calligraphy was not taught. Nevertheless, Deng was so attracted to the subject that he found himself a teacher. Ironically, a few years later it was his skill as a calligrapher, not his knowledge of English, that secured him his first job as a clerk in a court, where he was reputedly able to transcribe the proceedings at great speed, or as the Chinese said more colourfully, 'at a rate of ten thousand characters a day'.

What made Deng outstanding, however, was not his speed or originality, but his ability to imitate the styles of great masters – for example, the running script of Wang Xizhi (303–361), the cursive script of Sun Guoting (648–703) and of the monk Huaisu (725–785), and the clerical script of Yi Bingshou (1754–1815) – as well as an innovative form of seal script developed by his teacher, Xiao Tiean (1875–1958), which emphasized the horizontal rather than the vertical.

The Shanghai of the 1930s was the perfect milieu for Deng. By then his work was renowned for the boldness of its execution and its firmness of line, while at the same time he somehow managed to make his characters seem to float on the paper. As a calligrapher, Deng was also expected to be a good poet and this posed a problem for him. He had neither a good classical education nor a poetic temperament. He overcame the difficulty by secretly relying on the poetry of his talented friend Zao Weifang.

Deng's elegant classically-inspired works found ready purchasers among the rich, who sought sanctuary in the International Settlement of Shanghai as the Japanese stepped up their attacks on China. Deng shrewdly reinvested a portion of his profits in cultivating the local press. The journalists found Deng a far more refreshing and modern personality than his more traditionally-minded competitors. In particular, they loved the colourful

74 Having been a star in Shanghai in the 1930s, Deng Sanmu moved to Beijing in the mid-1950s to write books promoting the new, simplified Chinese characters.

Detail of fig. 75

exhibitions of his work that he staged, which they described as having the excitement of great religious festivals.

Like many other well-to-do people in the city, Deng kept open house; unlike them, however, he expected his guests to pour their own drinks, make their own tea and light their own cigarettes, leaving him to get on with his work. But once he had a drink in his hand he would hold forth on any topic that took his fancy, as if no one else were present.

Deng's eccentricity was another manifestation of his dislike of what he called the 'Gentlemanly Society' (*Zeng Pai*), which he felt was the cause of many of China's ills. He even founded a 'Crying Society' to lament China's woes. Those woes became all the more heart-rending when, in 1941, the Japanese finally seized the International Settlement in Shanghai. In an attempt to curry favour with the local community, they tried to persuade Deng to head the calligraphy society. His staunch refusal was widely admired by his compatriots, as was his habit of giving the money from the sale of his works to the poor.

In 1950 Shanghai's first Communist mayor, Chen Yi (pp. 91–9), made a special effort to win over the city's intellectuals to the New China. Deng's unsocialist outlook and cantankerous temperament were so pronounced, however, that he was difficult to accommodate. Eventually, in 1955, he was offered a well-paid post at the Educational Press in Beijing, writing out books in large characters to assist children with their reading and writing. He also helped promote the use of the new 'simplified' characters.

After his lean years in Shanghai, Deng was delighted by the good life he could now afford to enjoy in Beijing. Tongue in cheek, he even wrote poems praising socialism. But the good times did not last long. When the 'Hundred Flowers Movement' came in 1956–7, Deng openly expressed his views. With his legendary directness, he castigated both the Party and the Government for not paying enough attention to calligraphy. Within months he had been branded a 'Rightist', sacked and made unemployable.

It was in these circumstances that Deng created a pair of scrolls for a close friend (fig. 75). The text lamented their separation and bemoaned the way in which China's most talented people had been 'gathered up' in the anti-Rightist movement. Deng's right wrist had been troubling him for some time, but he managed, using his left hand, to develop a new style of cursive script, which was tinged with an aura of antiquity. He used this script to write out the following poem:

The wild geese fly south again.
　Startled, I sigh at how fast the months and years flow by.

Although we are separated,
  as if at the furthest corners of the earth,
  we shall always remember each other.

Because the sea perch and the brasenia
  are fresh and full of flavour
  They have all been gathered up
  by the fishermen and the woodcutters.

If I am about to write out poetry,
  with wine by my side,
  with whom could I really share such a pleasure still...
  but you?

On this pair of scrolls Deng added four seals, two on each, which demonstrate why many experts rank him among China's greatest seal carvers. On the first scroll, one of the seals shows two characters that recall the words of Zhuangzi:

If the heart is emptied of all worldly thoughts,
  then it becomes pure,
Like the brightness of sunlight
  in an empty house.

The other seal on the first scroll, which Deng had carved in 1938, reads:

In vain, I try to stir their senses.

The second scroll contains some surprises. In the puritanical atmosphere of New China, Deng had found it prudent simply to sign his work with his proper name, but after being branded a 'Rightist' he reverted to type and used one of his old signatures, which can be translated as 'Old Man Manure in a mood of inspiration', or more simply as 'Happy Old Shit'. Beneath this signature Deng placed his 'Lord of the Shits' seal. On this scroll, however, he added a second seal, freshly carved, which suggested that in 1958 he had 'gone into a mountain', a phrase used in China to describe retreating to a monastery to meditate in seclusion. This is almost certainly a reference to his banishment for being a 'Rightist'.

Deng's love of breaking with convention can also be seen in the unusual way he positions the characters on the paper in this work. Instead of placing the dedication on the outer right-hand side of the pair of scrolls and the signature on the outer left-hand side, he has written them side by side in the lower centre of the pair, thus creating a novel and interesting composition.

102

75 In 1958 Deng executed this pair of scrolls, whose dramatic, almost unreadable, wild cursive script helps conceal their meaning.

The story of the acquisition of this piece of calligraphy is one that Deng would have relished. In October 1970, I visited the Friendship Shop in the grounds of the British Consulate in Shanghai, which the Red Guards had seized in 1967. The shop was full of costumes from the Shanghai Opera, as well as other works of art that were being sold off in a fit of revolutionary fervour. The man who showed me Deng's scrolls urged me to buy them, emphasizing that they were exceptional. Once they were in my possession and I had found out what they said, I could not help but think that the man had been sufficiently well educated not only to read the calligraphy, but also to understand the classical language that Deng had used. He no doubt felt that having these scrolls purchased by a foreigner was better than letting them remain in Shanghai, where they risked destruction if anyone else became aware of their inner meaning.

Of course, Deng's seal claiming that he had been meditating in seclusion was a euphemism for a situation that was in fact a great deal less romantic. Without a job, and there being no market for calligraphy, he was having to eke out an existence by carving seals. But because the use of his right hand was impaired, he had to resort to using his left hand. The rather strange, strong characters Deng carved seemed to reflect his formidable spirit of old, while his occasional use of the new simplified characters gave some of his seals a modern flavour.

Although most of the seals Deng produced were for fellow artists, some government and Party officials were willing to turn a blind eye to his political stigma when they wanted a small masterpiece on the cheap. Soon, however, Deng's financial problems were compounded by poor health. His years of heavy drinking had led to a condition that necessitated the amputation of one of his legs in 1961 – after which he signed himself 'One Leg'. Two years later, he died of stomach cancer.

In 1980, seventeen years after his death, Deng, along with most others who had been condemned as 'Rightists' in 1958, had his name cleared. As part of the process of making amends, a retrospective exhibition of his work was staged in Shanghai. The praise for his achievements was effusive, ranking him as the greatest Chinese calligrapher of the twentieth century and one of the greatest seal carvers of all time.

One of the people who saw the exhibition was Chen Lei, the governor of Heilongjiang province. In 1983, following the death of the Dengs' only child, a daughter, Chen Lei persuaded Deng's wife to donate all of her husband's material to Harbin, the capital of his province. It was agreed that, in return, a special Deng Sanmu museum would be established and Mrs Deng would be looked after comfortably in her old age.

By 1986 Chen Lei was no longer the governor and no museum had been established. Finally, it was arranged that a gallery would be opened within the Provincial Museum in Harbin. Guo Kuoyu, a scholar and one of Deng's former students, was invited to catalogue the material and arrange the first exhibition. Deng's collection remains in Harbin, but poor Mrs Deng never had her part of the bargain honoured.

Deng was one of the first Chinese calligraphers to feel entirely comfortable in the modern world. Though not a scholar, he was a truly professional artist. As such, he helped clear the way for the present generation of Neo-Classical calligraphers – none of whom has yet matched his colourful eccentricity.

MAO ZEDONG

1893–1976

The revolutionary Classicist

One of the many tantalizing aspects of Mao's personality is that this most revolutionary of Chinese leaders was so passionate about the classical art of calligraphy. Like the emperors who had ruled China before him, he used calligraphy both as a source of solace and as an attribute of power. But none of his predecessors had ever been able to mould the art of calligraphy into such a potent instrument of political will.

A passion for calligraphy

Mao's passion for calligraphy and the classics had its roots in the cultural values of his generation. In order to be regarded as educated and cultured, a man had to excel in both these subjects. For Mao, calligraphy and the classics fulfilled different needs. Calligraphy was 'an active pastime – always a way of strengthening the mind and body while attaining tranquillity'. He felt that, unlike other arts, it used 'the entire body to express the writer's spirit'. The literary and historical classics, on the other hand, covered the vast sweep of China's heritage, at times in extraordinarily beautiful language.

Traditionally, Chinese calligraphers cultivated their art in quiet studios well equipped with large tables and different types of paper, and a wide variety of brushes, inksticks, inkstones and seals. Starting out as a poor

105

student and then being engaged in fighting and directing military operations for twenty years, Mao developed his talent for calligraphy in very different circumstances. He did not have the full panoply of brushes used by serious calligraphers and he had to be economical in his use of paper, which was often in short supply.

During Mao's years on the Long March (1934–5) and while he was in the Communist stronghold of Yanan (1935–47), most of his calligraphy was run-of-the-mill work, such as drafts, reports and official letters that had to be produced in a legible hand. Sometimes he wrote slogans and inscriptions in support of his policies. These, too, had to be written clearly if they were to be widely understood.

Although Mao derived great satisfaction from using a brush, he also frequently followed the recently introduced fashions of using a pen or pencil and of writing from left to right, rather than from top to bottom. Because he repeatedly wrote in this way, Mao's calligraphy began to give greater emphasis to the horizontal dimension of a character than to the traditional vertical one. Mao also broke from tradition by not adding a seal after his signature, which he seems to have considered too elitist a practice for his own taste. (Later, he did use a seal in his books to show that they belonged to him.)

Most of his calligraphy was done with a hard-tipped brush, which was ideally suited to writing small characters quickly and clearly in running script. When using a brush with a very thin tip, he liked to make elongated downward strokes that were like silken threads, but when working with a thicker brush, he emphasized diagonal strokes in a determined manner. These were the hallmarks of his calligraphy even into his old age.

The calligraphy of Mao's letters is more revealing about his attitudes and moods than the slogans and inscriptions he produced for public display. The more relaxed he felt, the less pretentious was his brushwork. For example, a letter he wrote to one of his former teachers in 1936 was done in his 'best' writing, whereas the style he used for writing to subordinates in the Ninth Division in 1937 was elegant, relaxed and quietly authoritative, and was done from left to right in the modern way. Other pieces were more assertive.

After Mao had reached the sanctuary of Yanan in 1935, he would occasionally write out one of his poems for a colleague or someone else he wished to impress. The piece illustrated in fig. 77 is his poem *Huichang*, which Mao had composed in 1934, just before being forced to embark on the Long March. Its striking opening words, 'A new dawn breaks in the East', were intended to describe not only the beginning of a new day but

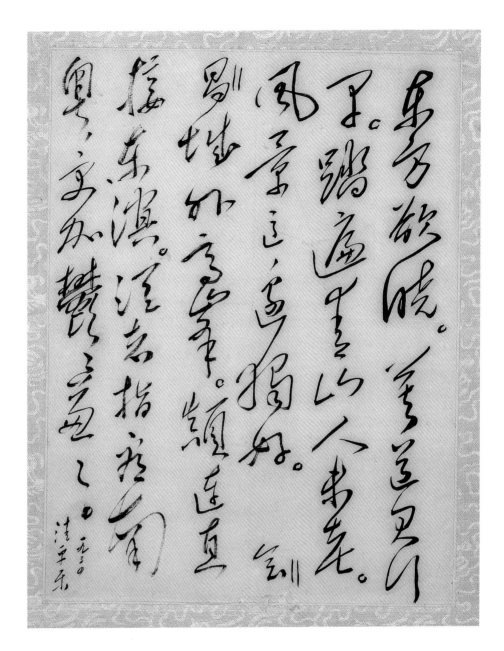

also the rising strength of the Communist forces who were striving to create a New China. His brushwork has a modest, scholarly air.

> *A new dawn breaks in the East.*
> > *Do not say 'You start too early';*
> > *crossing these blue hills adds nothing to one's years,*
> > *the landscape here is beyond compare.*
>
> *Straight from the walls of Huichang's lofty peaks,*
> > *range after range, extend to the eastern seas.*
>
> *Our soldiers point south to Guangdong,*
> > *looming lusher and greener in the distance.*

As Mao came closer to victory over the Nationalist forces, the style of his calligraphy began to change. Not only did his running script become lighter and freer, but it was noticeable that he was beginning to juxtapose large characters with small ones, notably in his masthead for the *People's Daily*, the Communist Party newspaper established in 1946. This was the first example of Mao's calligraphy to become widely known, and one which amply demonstrated that he had developed his own calligraphic aesthetic. When showing the four characters (*Renmin Ribao*) to a colleague, he remarked that 'the two characters in the middle are smaller and the two at each end a little larger, as that makes the masthead prettier'.

Mao was not alone among the Communist leaders in his passion for poetry and calligraphy. But to a greater extent than any of his cultured colleagues, he believed that China's classical histories contained the secrets of political power. In the summer of 1949 he based himself in the Fragrant Hills, some thirty kilometres to the west of Beijing, from where he planned to direct the final phase of the defeat of Jiang Jieshi (Chiang Kaishek). The lessons he had learnt from the histories had helped bring him to the verge of power. Now he needed to understand how to rule and how to keep the power he had won, to which end he read and reread the classical texts that analysed these issues so trenchantly. This thorough grounding in Chinese history and literature increasingly imbued his poetry with classical and epic qualities.

Although it was not reported during his lifetime, one of the strongest indications of his passion for calligraphy was the reading material he took with him when he set out from Beijing in January 1950 on a ten-day train journey to Moscow for his first meeting with Joseph Stalin. The main item was the thirty-seven-volume *Sanxi Tang Fatie*, which contained copies of the most famous pieces of calligraphy that had been held in the Imperial Collection during the reign of the Qian Long emperor (1736–95). Mao studied these volumes because he believed that fine calligraphy enhanced the prestige of any Chinese ruler, be he imperial or revolutionary.

Victory itself brought changes. Now that the revolution had proved a success, Mao had to settle down to the task of building a New China. This did not preclude him from enjoying the fruits of victory, many of which for him were cultural. In his new quarters in the leadership compound set alongside Zhongnanhai lake, his library of the Chinese classics expanded rapidly. Mao could easily have had a proper calligrapher's studio, replete with a large table and stacks of paper of various sizes. But because he was so tightly locked into his habit of writing small characters on small pieces of paper, he did not feel that this was necessary. He did, however, celebrate becoming the ruler of China by acquiring some goat's-hair brushes, which gave his calligraphy a softer line.

Calligraphy in New China

Although Mao loved calligraphy, he knew that the culture which had nurtured the art was a major impediment to his plans for bringing about a far-reaching socialist revolution in China. Publicly, he played down the significance of calligraphy, but at the same time he used it both to cloak himself with an imperial aura and as a source of personal comfort.

By the time Mao won control of China, he was already a rather lonely figure. He saw himself as China's great leader – a man who had colleagues, but not friends. His sense of isolation was compounded by a deep distrust of his colleagues, who were intent on marginalizing him, as well as by his difficulties with Jiang Qing, his third wife. To make matters worse, he found his new lifestyle highly restrictive, especially as he was obliged to have a full security guard every time he went outside the leadership compound. But Mao's brush and his poetic imagination helped fill the emotional void. He would bury himself in his calligraphy for hours at a time.

In 1955 he instructed his staff to start collecting rubbings and photographs of inscriptions by earlier masters that had been carved in stone, as these were often the only surviving examples of their works. Within a few years they had amassed several hundred such items for him. Mao also spent a great deal of time studying the original works that were in the Palace Museum and in other collections still in private hands.

Calligraphy was a personal hobby which Mao liked to share with people he admired and by whom he did not feel threatened. When saying goodbye to Party colleagues, he never escorted them to the door or to their cars, but he always accorded this respect to his poet-calligrapher friends. These included Liu Yazi and Ye Gongchuo (pp. 74–9), both of whom were former leading members of the Nationalist Party. In 1950 Mao wrote the name plaque for Liu's new home in Beijing, 'The House of Heaven on Earth', a name by no means lived up to by the comforts it provided. Even though Ye had been declared a 'Rightist' in 1957, Mao still invited him to his birthday party later that year.

Showing his calligraphic skills

Not surprisingly, the place in which Mao made his mark most clearly was the capital city. The first institution to be blessed with his calligraphy was Beijing University, where Mao had been a librarian in the 1920s, which received a new name plaque in 1950.

Within a few years, Mao's calligraphy was emblazoned on new public buildings across the city. The most prominent was the Memorial to the

Martyrs of the Revolution, the focal point of the newly enlarged Tiananmen Square, which was unveiled on 1 May 1958. Mao's inscription marked a major break with convention. He wrote in a running script. rather than the more formal styles traditionally used on memorials and plaques, and, in keeping with his long-established practice, he did not add a seal after his signature. He also provided the name plaques for the Museum of Chinese History (on the eastern side of the Square), the Museum of Military History, Beijing Railway Station, the Minorities Cultural Palace and the Workers' Park. Less predictably, Mao's calligraphy graced the entrance to a Middle School not far from Tiananmen Square – the one that his daughter attended.

Whenever Mao wrote out the characters for a municipal name plaque he did so on small sheets of paper, which craftsmen then projected through a 'magic lantern' to achieve the required enlargement. Most of these inscriptions were executed without difficulty and to his satisfaction. The commission that caused him the greatest trouble was the plaque for the China Art Gallery (*Zhong Guo Mei Shu Guan*), which he did in 1963. It took him several hours just to produce what he considered a satisfactory version of *Zhong*, meaning 'middle' or 'China', the first and simplest of the five characters. Perhaps Mao felt intimidated by the fact that his calligraphy was going to be placed above the entrance to a building in which China's finest contemporary art would be displayed.

From time to time Mao's slogans and inscriptions appeared in the Chinese press. Covering a remarkable range of subjects, they usually urged people to make greater efforts, expressed hopes for continued unity among the people, or celebrated successes that had been achieved or to which

Mao aspired. These pieces were often reproduced as woodblock-printed facsimiles by Rong Bao Zhai, the main art shop in Beijing.

By the late 1950s Mao had begun to take a serious interest in cursive script – especially 'wild' cursive script, the mastery of which requires great talent and skill. In particular, he devoted much effort to studying the work of the 'mad monk' Huaisu (725–785) and of Zhang Xu (active 710–750). This script was ideally suited to expressing power and venting frustration and anger, all of which Mao had in abundance. Moreover, there was not a politician or artist alive who had been able to master this genre of the calligraphic art.

Mao's first public offering in bold cursive script consisted of the two characters *Hong Qi* ('Red Flag'), which he wrote in 1958 as the masthead for the Party's new journal dealing with the theoretical aspects of Marxism-Leninism (fig. 78). Later, he explained how he had made several attempts to give these characters the flair that he felt they deserved. The version he liked best had been inspired by the image of a girl performing the 'red silk dance'. The first part of the character for 'red' was produced in one stroke, like the silk in the dancer's hand, which has a rhythm that flows and yet conveys rapid movement. In commenting on his work, Mao said that he had 'painted' these two characters, rather than written them. The choice of this word indicates the importance he attached to the image he was seeking to convey.

As Mao studied calligraphy more intensively and practised ever harder to enhance his skills, he developed several different styles. His choice of which to use depended on whether he was writing official correspondence, producing inscriptions or slogans for publication, or writing more personally in prose or poetry. As his technique improved, he increasingly used his calligraphy to enhance his authority and prestige across the country and to intimidate his subordinates.

After 1959 Mao's calligraphy seems to have become even more self-consciously intimidating – *baqi*, as the Chinese say. In 1965, for instance, he wrote a letter to Guo Moruo (pp. 80–90), China's leading cultural figure at the time, in which some of the calligraphy is so flamboyant that it suggests that Mao intended to demonstrate that he was not only a powerful figure, but also a better calligrapher even than Guo.

Although Mao's inscriptions on public buildings and his slogans that appeared in the press were of an increasingly high standard, what really made his name as a calligrapher were the renditions he did of his own poems (figs 79 and 80), which he used to great effect in building up his cult of personality. This process started slowly with the publication of a few of

Detail of fig. 79

111

his poems in 1957. Then in 1963 he published a collection of thirty-seven poems he had written over the preceding thirty-five years. The powerful imagery and classical style of these pieces emphasized his historic achievements and national pride. Only one was truly personal, and that was about the loss of his first wife. Sales boomed.

The calligraphic versions of several of these poems that Mao published over the next two years demonstrated that he was an extraordinarily talented calligrapher, and arguably better than almost all his imperial predecessors. The publication in 1962 of his poem *Mount Liupan* aroused interest because of its content. He had composed it in 1935 to record the crossing of this mountain chain, which was one of the great triumphs of the Long March. It included the famous lines:

We who have already marched so many thousand miles,
we are not men if we now fail to reach the Great Wall.

The appearance of this poem at a time when the Chinese were still enduring great hardship as a result of the ill-conceived Great Leap Forward was widely seen in China as Mao's effort to remind both his colleagues and the people of the heroic achievements of earlier days, and to impress on them the need for continued stamina. Among those interested in calligraphy, however, excitement over the poem had less to do with its content than with the dramatic form of wild cursive script in which Mao had rendered it.

The styles of calligraphy in which Mao wrote out his thirty-seven poems vary enormously. His *Reply to Mr Liu Yazi* (1950) and the poem he wrote about *Beidaihe*, the coastal resort he visited every summer, are both notable for being in his most relaxed style of brushwork. All of his poems dealing with the great moments of recent Chinese history in which he had played a leading part were executed in a wild cursive script full of a power and excitement befitting the events they recorded (fig. 79).

79 Mao's poem *The Long March* (1935) is a song of triumph recording the extraordinary hardship which the Red Armies overcame as they struggled to escape from the Nationalist forces and reach the Communist sanctuary of Yanan:

... Making light ten thousand crags and torrents...
The three armies march on, each face glowing.

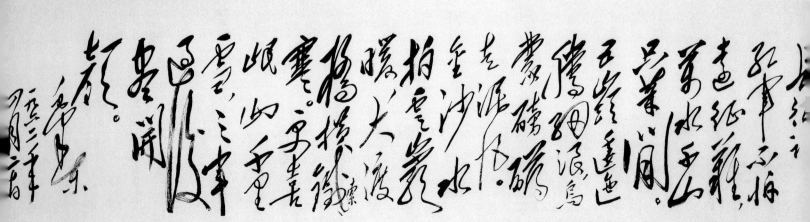

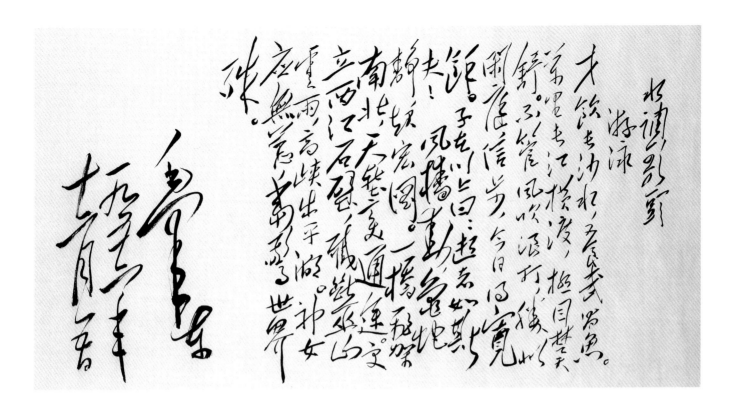

80 Mao's poem *Swimming* (1956) is one of the few in which he expressed personal pleasure:

Now I am swimming across the great Yangzi river...
Better by far than idly strolling in a courtyard. Today I am at ease.

Mao's calligraphic rendering of this piece is regarded by many Chinese calligraphers as reflecting the spirit of an exceptionally cultured person. It was this poem that he chose to write out and give as a present to Viscount Montgomery when he visited China in 1961.

Calligraphy and the Cultural Revolution

From the autumn of 1962, Mao was once again setting the political agenda. Up to that point he had allowed his colleagues to introduce reforms that he disliked but accepted as necessary. However, as soon as he suspected that these reforms were leading towards the decollectivization of agriculture, he began his preparations to stop what he saw as the 'return to the capitalist road'.

At this time Mao was also preoccupied with the Sino-Soviet dispute, which was becoming increasingly tense. His defiant poem known as *Manjianghong* (1963) was widely regarded as a statement of his conviction that China would prevail in its dispute with the Soviet Union over the future direction of the international Communist movement. It contains the much-quoted phrase 'Time presses – seize the day, seize the hour'. In retrospect, however, the poem also appears to have been a ringing condemnation of the large number of his colleagues who Mao believed shared the 'revisionist' attitudes espoused by the Soviet leadership.

Not only were the calligraphic versions of Mao's poems now extensively available in book and poster form, but he also began to wield his brush on the mastheads of China's newspapers, all of which were controlled by the Party. In 1964 alone, he wrote new mastheads for most of the main provincial newspapers as part of his increasingly active preparations for reasserting his authority. Then in the summer of 1966, when he judged that circumstances were ripe, Mao struck out at his unsuspecting colleagues

113

by inaugurating the so-called 'Great Proletarian Cultural Revolution' (generally known simply as the 'Cultural Revolution').

At the beginning of the Cultural Revolution, Mao was quick to portray himself as a writer of 'big-character posters'. On 5 August 1966, during the eleventh plenum of the Eighth Party Congress, he unleashed on the Party the slogan: 'Bombard the Headquarters – My first big-character poster'. Shortly thereafter, posters appeared showing Mao holding a massive brush dripping with red ink – like a bloody dagger – and bearing the slogan in his own calligraphy (see fig. 42 on p. 49). This slogan opened the way for the Red Guards to attack those whom Mao saw as his rivals within the leadership, which meant the majority of them, including Liu Shaoqi (the president) and Deng Xiaoping (the secretary-general of the Party).

As the Cultural Revolution gathered momentum, Mao's calligraphy began to appear everywhere. Tens of millions of 'Little Red Books' were published, containing Mao's slogans and poems in calligraphic as well as printed form. Huge posters were printed and pasted up in public places. Thousands of the statues of Mao that had been erected across the country were adorned with his calligraphy, engraved on concrete or stone. The finest reproductions of his work were the large woodblock prints produced at Rong Bao Zhai.

By the latter part of the Cultural Revolution, Mao was close to eighty years of age and in failing health. Little new calligraphy by him appeared in print. His last inscription, written with an enfeebled hand, was produced in 1974 for the Beijing Foreign Languages Institute.

Following Mao's death in 1976 and the ousting of the Gang of Four a month later, the amount of Mao's calligraphy that was on public display declined rapidly. The 'Little Red Books' and wall posters were soon gone. Then, as China under Deng Xiaoping began to concentrate on economic reform, most of the statues of Mao and their accompanying calligraphy erected during the Cultural Revolution were removed. The huge enlargements of his poems also disappeared as modernization progressed. In the mid-1990s one of the last and most prominently displayed pieces of his calligraphy, his poem *Mount Liupan*, was removed from Shanghai Airport when it was redesigned to accommodate a shopping mall and duty-free shops (see fig. 41 on p. 48).

In 1993, on the centenary of Mao's birth, the authorities published a large collection of his calligraphy, with the title inscription written by President Jiang Zemin. Its ten volumes contained more than 2,500 pages of material. The collection was not comprehensive, however. It was particularly noticeable that it contained none of his Cultural Revolutionary works. This is hardly surprising, since the aim of the authorities was to honour Mao's achievements, not to examine his weaknesses and the darker side of his character. Nevertheless, for those who understood calligraphy, this collection was revealing about Mao the man.

Revelations of the brush

The published collection of Mao's calligraphy contains reproductions of 233 classical poems that he wrote out in his own hand. If the date of each piece of calligraphy were printed alongside it, this would throw an interesting light on Mao's state of mind over the years. His mood when he wrote each piece can be deduced both from the content of the particular poem he chose to write out and from tell-tale signs in the brushwork that indicate

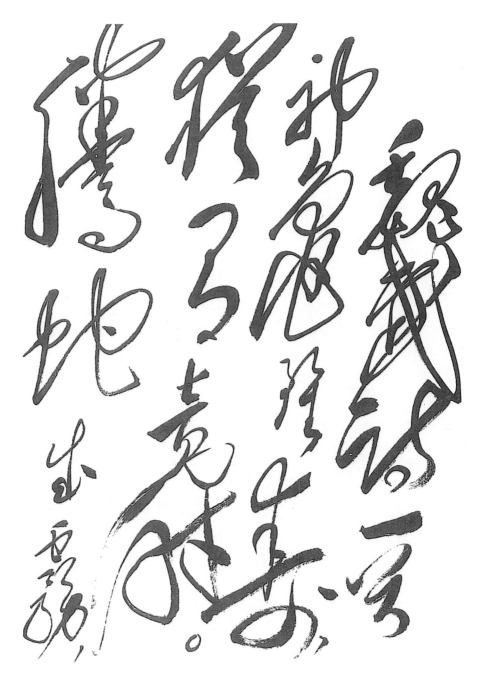

whether he was relaxed or tense when he did so. Unfortunately, only two of the items in the collection appear with a date, but they give a glimpse of what might have been revealed if all had been dated.

The first dated piece is *The Song of Mount Lu* by Li Bai (701–762). Lushan (as Mount Lu is better known) was seared into Mao's memory because it was the location of the 1959 Party Conference, at which Mao had thwarted criticism of his Great Leap Forward by Marshal Peng Dehuai – the most serious split in the Chinese leadership since 1949. In 1961 the agricultural situation in China was so bad that Mao was forced to back down and, in essence, agree to dismantle the People's Communes. On 16 September of that year he wrote out Li Bai's poem, which contains the lines:

> *I care not what people say,*
>> *I begin to know the Way*
> *I see from far immortals in the cloudy land...*
>
> *I'll go before you somewhere beyond the ninth sphere*
>> *and wait for you to wander in the zenith clear.*

Mao's brushwork is relaxed, indeed almost smug with self-satisfaction, and his choice of poetry is revealing. It reflects his conviction that he is the great leader and the one who knows what to do. A year later, at the tenth plenum of the Party, he insisted that his colleagues should never forget the class struggle.

The other dated poem is *The Indomitable Soul* (fig. 81) by the Chinese ruler Cao Cao (155–220), whom Mao, unlike most Chinese historians, greatly admired. Mao wrote out this poem on 30 December 1962, the day he declared his uncompromising line that was to lead him to launch the Cultural Revolution. His brushwork is very different from that in *The Song of Mount Lu*. It looks as if he was boldly slashing his way through the poem with his brush, although some of the tight twists and turns do suggest a trace of anxiety. Ten days later, Mao wrote the equally defiant poem *Manjianghong*.

On another occasion, he wrote out the poem by Li Bai entitled *Invitation to Wine*, which contains such memorable lines as:

> *How many great men were forgotten through the ages?*
>> *Great drinkers are better known than sober sages.*

and

> *I only want to get drunk and never wake.*

At one level Li Bai's poem is about friendship and wine, but at another it is about depression. Some of Mao's brushwork brings to mind the flashes of knives and swords on a battlefield, suggesting that at the time he wrote this piece he was both depressed and angry.

It was probably in a similar mood that he chose to write out the poem *Reply to Bai Juyi* by Liu Yuxi (772–843), which contains the lines:

> *In native land, I look like human debris.*
> *A thousand sails pass by the side of sunken ships...*
> *Today I hear you chant the praise of comradeship,*
> *I wish this cup of wine might well inspire me.*

In this piece Mao's brushwork is combative and feisty, as if to help him set his fears into perspective.

One of the most striking pieces of Mao's calligraphy among all those published is a haunting couplet by Jia Dao (779–843). It was written to a friend who had left Chang'an, the Tang capital, earlier in the year to travel to Fujian province. Although it was now autumn, nothing had been heard from him. The verse conveys a sense of nervousness and loneliness. No date is given for Mao's rendering of it, but on stylistic grounds his piece was probably done in the early to mid-1960s. Some Chinese calligraphers say that the juddering brushwork is an intentional play on the style of the eccentric calligraphers of the Ming dynasty, while others see in it the nervous, shaky hand of a sad and lonely man. (Han Yu wrote a similar piece, see pp. 213–14.) Whatever the explanation, the subject of the couplet is maudlin.

> *The autumn wind blows across the River Wei*
> *and falling leaves cover Chang'an.*

Mao's calligraphy is genuinely admired by leading calligraphers living in China today. They regard it as a rare and potent mixture of the talented brush of a fine artist and the élan of a historic figure writing about the epic revolutionary events of his lifetime in his own classical poetry. But Mao's influence on modern calligraphy is another matter altogether. The main message that many young calligraphers have drawn from Mao's style is that they, too, can be a law unto themselves and do not need to follow the 'rules' of calligraphy. This would not be a bad influence, had they Mao's poetic inspiration and consummate skill with the brush.

4 BREAKING THE MOULD

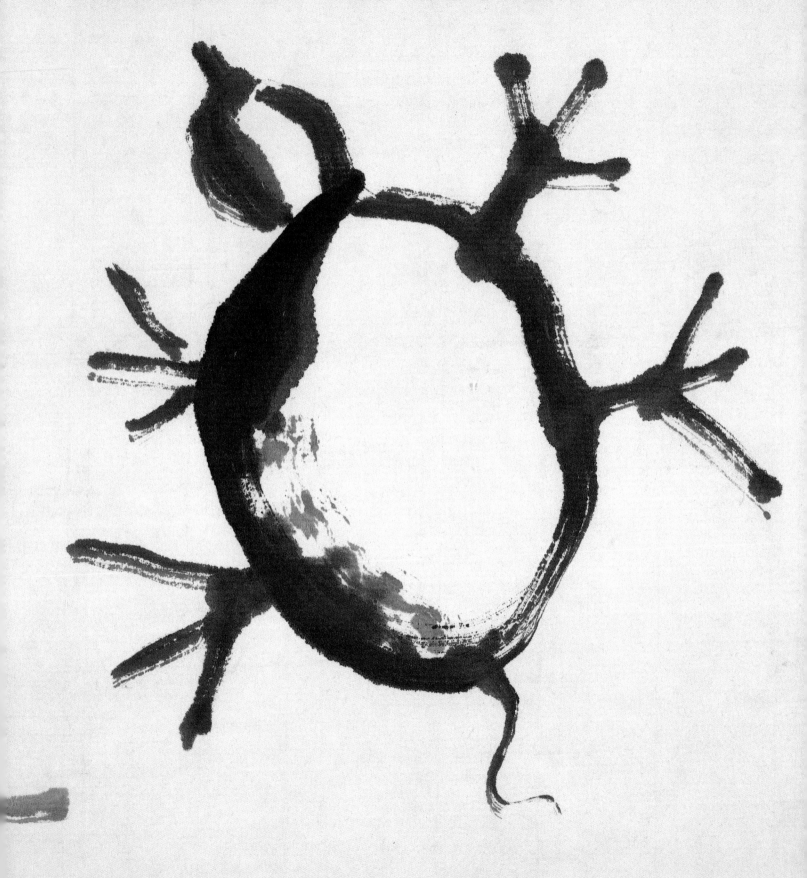

ZHANG ZHENGYU

1904–76

The theatrical designer who revolutionized calligraphy

82 Zhang's career took him from being a theatrical designer in Shanghai in the 1930s, to choreographing massive revolutionary parades in Beijing in the 1950s, and then to transforming the ancient art of calligraphy in the 1960s and 1970s.

The great parades in Beijing were one of the few colourful aspects of the New China of the 1950s. Although predominantly revolutionary in tone, they were visually sumptuous and carefully choreographed events. No one who saw them would ever have thought that the man masterminding these productions would soon be instilling new life into ancient styles of calligraphy.

Breaking the rules

In some respects, Zhang Zhengyu was an unlikely candidate for this role. While growing up in Wuxi, in Jiangsu province, he had received a thorough grounding in calligraphy. What really fascinated him, however, were the modern arts of cosmopolitan Shanghai. In his twenties and thirties he succeeded in making his name there as a cartoonist, as well as by wielding his brush as a designer of costumes and sets for theatrical productions and films. He was also successful as a painter of animals, birds, flowers and still lifes. As he travelled around China as a refugee during the war, his paintings began to absorb some of the influence of folk art, the vitality of which impressed him deeply.

As was so often the case in China, it was the political events of the day that set the course of Zhang's career and his subsequent artistic development. In addition to being in charge of the great spectacles in Beijing in the early 1950s, he was the artistic director of private performances staged for Mao and the other Party leaders. But even Mao's liking for these events did not save Zhang from almost being declared a 'Rightist' in 1957. Shaken by this experience, he began to retreat from public life and devote more time to his painting.

Zhang was fascinated by cats. Those he painted did not have the sentimental appearance usually favoured by Chinese artists, but were lively ones that looked more like calligraphy with fur. With his cartoonist's eye he captured an amazing range of feline expressions: some rather sinister, others that made people smile or even hoot with laughter. After his retirement Zhang produced many such paintings, greatly encouraged by the high prices that Japanese tourists were willing to pay for them.

Zhang also began to focus his energy on finding ways to revitalize calligraphy, an art which he felt had languished for too long within the straitjacket of Chinese convention. The freedom of design he had developed in the course of his theatrical work and in his painting gave him the vision to use a brush in ways traditional calligraphers had never dared.

In the mid-1960s Zhang made his great breakthrough in developing a new style. He did this by writing a number of small seal characters in running script, a technique that had first been tried during the Ming dynasty but had never really developed. The forms of the characters themselves reflected the fact that they had originally been carved, so they tended to be neat, even somewhat dull. In calligraphic terms, what Zhang was doing was an artistic contradiction, but it gave the ancient form of small seal script a new vitality. It was in this style that he began to show his real skill in moulding characters into an overall decorative composition. He was more enthused by the overall vigour of a composition than by the structure of its individual characters and their strokes.

The content of Zhang's calligraphy in this style ranged from classical poems to the works of Mao. Sometimes he would use one of Mao's graphic but less political couplets as his text. For example, in one work he used the lines: 'The eagle strikes up towards the heights of Heaven, the fish dives down into the depths of the water.' On other occasions he would take more political phrases out of context. For example, in his 1963 poem widely known as *Manjianghong* ('The Whole River is Red') Mao had included the words 'The Four Seas are rising, wind and thunder roaring' as one of a crescendo of phrases conveying the idea that nothing could stop China from becoming the leader of the international Communist movement, which was then still headed by the Soviet Union. When Zhang used this phrase on its own, however, it was open to different interpretations. It could be read, for instance, as meaning that the turbulent dawn of a new era was at hand, though without any indication as to what this might entail.

Zhang delighted in the scope for personal expression that was provided by ambiguity. In one of his works he used subtle wording to reject the idea that politics should be allowed to overshadow literature. In another he used the same device to convey his belief that it was better to pursue scholarship for its own sake, rather than as a means of attaining high political office.

By 1966 Zhang feared that he might not be able to indulge in such pleasures for much longer, having had a premonition that something terrible would soon occur (fig. 83). As the atmosphere worsened that summer, with China moving inexorably towards the horrors of the Cultural

83 In early 1966 Zhang skilfully used classical idioms to express his concern that something terrible was about to happen in China.

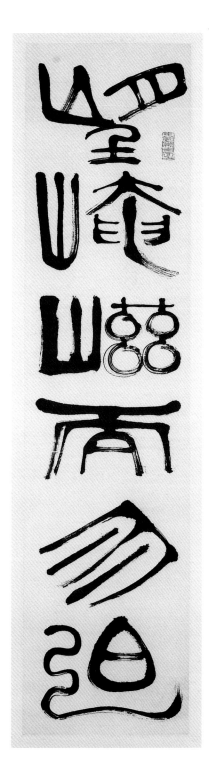

Revolution, Zhang created this couplet from two separate lines of the *Li Sao*, by Qu Yuan (340–278 BC):

I look West towards Mount Yanzi, but do not proceed,
Afraid that the shrike will sing before the equinox,
showing that all Nature has gone awry.

In Chinese mythology Mount Yanzi is where the sun sets and is therefore associated with death. This couplet had been used by the great twentieth-century writer Lu Xun to mean that he must hurry on with his work before it was too late. This may also have been the sense in which Zhang used it. But he might have meant that things were going wrong and he wanted time to stand still so that they did not get worse. Whatever the explanation, the sense of concern is clear. Zhang gave the scrolls to his friend Yang Xianyi, who had had a similar premonition.

During the Cultural Revolution, Zhang, along with several of his friends, including Huang Miaozi and his wife Yu Feng, was condemned as 'a ghost and a monster'. The main charge against them was that when they had been living in Chongqing during the war they had been members of a cultural club, which in reality had been an anti-Communist organization. The Gang of Four added, with the perverse logic of the Cultural Revolution, that in Zhang's case his passion for painting cats (*mao* in Chinese) was a manifestation of anti-Maoist sentiment.

All those accused of being 'ghosts and monsters' were treated roughly by the Red Guards, and Zhang was no exception. Instead of being beaten to death, driven to suicide or imprisoned, however, he was sent to a State farm. In 1972, after five years' hard labour, he was allowed to return to Beijing. At home, he discreetly painted innocuous pictures and worked on his calligraphy; outside, he would meet up with his friends and admirers, with whom he often drowned his sorrows in alcohol.

Developing new techniques

Over the next four years Zhang recovered his rich sense of humour and irony. At the same time he resumed the development of his calligraphy, which had been curtailed during his years in the countryside. His calligraphy became highly innovative as he began blending the pictograms taken from ancient bronze objects (*zhongding wen*) with seal-script characters that had been carved into stone. Appropriately, he named his studio 'The Pavilion of Characters Carved on Bronze and Stone'.

This new style enabled him to create more imaginative and powerful compositions. He especially liked to produce contrasts between the initially

121

heavy, ink-laden strokes of a wet brush and the drier ones that followed, with the hairs of the brush separating to create several thinner, parallel lines or a granular effect as they skimmed across the surface of the paper.

Since the Cultural Revolution was still in full flow, Zhang was wisely cautious about what he wrote. He knew that Jiang Qing, Mao's wife, was particularly keen to expose any artists she suspected of being unsound in matters of revolutionary art. Fortunately, as Zhang liked Mao's poetry he could quite easily find words by him that he enjoyed rendering in his own calligraphy. Even within these constraints of content, he could still find allusions through which to express his feelings (fig. 84).

In his later years Zhang took delight in working in wild cursive script at great speed. One day in the early 1970s he was so pleased with a piece he had just finished that he turned to his young friend Gu Gan and exclaimed, 'This is even better than the work of Huaisu!' (a seventh-century monk who was one of the most famous practitioners of that style, and the one on whom Mao modelled his calligraphy).

It was in this same powerful wild cursive script that, five days after Zhou Enlai's death on 8 January 1976, Zhang wrote out a poem that had been composed by his son-in-law. In it he gave vent to his grief:

> *Not only is all of China in tears,*
> *the whole world, too, laments.*
> *In three thousand years of recorded history,*
> *how many figures like you have we seen?*

In the early summer of that year, Zhang gave his greatest performance in wild cursive script. While he was on a visit to his old friends Huang Miaozi and Yu Feng, who had only recently been released from prison, all three of them were lamenting the death of Zhou Enlai and the continuing power of the Gang of Four, and consoling themselves with a great deal of wine. Suddenly, and much to Yu Feng's horror, Zhang leapt up, unfurled a very special length of paper that she had just acquired (measuring a metre wide and ten metres long) and began writing at speed. The more Zhang wrote, the less concerned Yu Feng became that he was going to waste her precious paper. She could see that he was writing out the two sets of ninety characters inscribed on the Da Guan Lou Pavilion, which stands by the side of a lake just outside Kunming. What he was doing amounted to not simply a compelling display of his powers of memory, but a veritable symphony of the calligraphic art (see fig. 21 on pp. 28–9).

The first part of the poem described the beautiful view that could be seen from the pavilion. The second part struck a far deeper chord, not only for

84 In his poem *Ode to a Plum Blossom* Mao made the point that China wanted a respected place in the international Communist movement. In producing his own calligraphic rendering of it, Zhang was probably indicating that he wanted to be respected in Chinese society.

Zhang but also for his host and hostess, who had been treated even more harshly than himself during the Cultural Revolution. It contrasted the heroic achievements of the past with the awfulness of the present, concluding with the words: 'But the stelae recording the exploits of our heroes of the past are cracked and broken, their ashes scattered.'

Some weeks later, in the early morning of 26 July 1976, an earthquake devastated the city of Tangshan. So severely did it shake buildings even in Beijing, 200 kilometres from its epicentre, that large numbers of people fled from their homes to camp in the streets. Zhang made up a simple bed for himself beneath the *Saphora japonica* trees that lined the pavement. In a piece of calligraphy that he wrote the next day he described waking up to find his bed half-covered with fallen leaves and the ground carpeted with a layer of white blossom. For Zhang the blossom recalled the white paper flowers the Chinese use at funerals – of which there would be so many after the earthquake. Though saddened by the huge loss of life, Zhang and his friends hoped that the earthquake was indeed the traditional Chinese omen that the ruling dynasty would soon be overthrown.

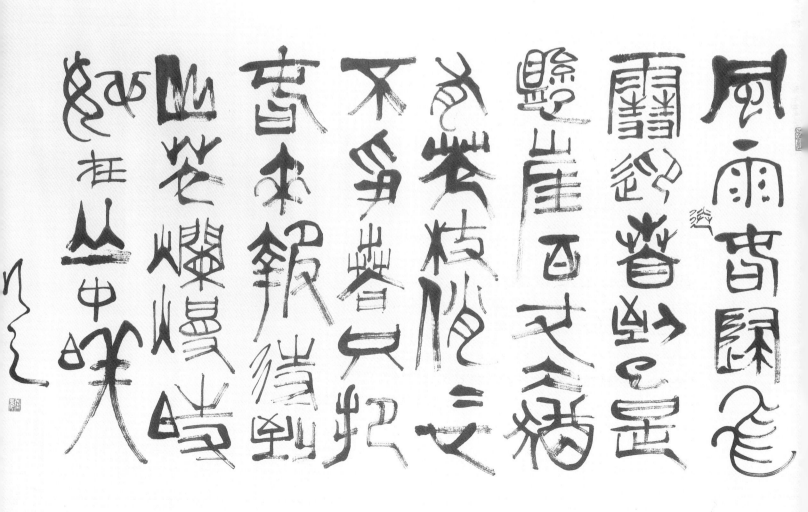

Death with satisfaction

Within six weeks Mao was dead. As Zhang lay in hospital suffering from cirrhosis of the liver, his misery was compounded by the thought that the Gang of Four might yet be able to seize power. But then, out of the blue, on 15 October Zhang's nephew brought him the news that the Gang of Four had been overthrown. Zhang's elation may have been too much for him, for within a day or so he had collapsed and died. One senses, however, that before he passed away he must have experienced a feeling of deep satisfaction that the Gang of Four were now in jail.

Among the works Zhang left behind was one that he did on New Year's Day 1976, a week before Zhou Enlai died. The text was a couplet by Mao that had been used in a poem by Marshal Ye Jianying. Aptly expressing Zhang's hope that the Gang of Four would be overthrown, it was to prove remarkably prophetic:

> *Nothing in the world is unachievable*
> *If you have the will to succeed.*

Indeed, it was the will of Marshal Ye which ten months later played a key role in the arrest of Jiang Qing and her supporters.

After Zhang's funeral his notoriously tightfisted wife went through all his effects. She was shocked to discover a small fortune in banknotes hidden among his books. This explained why Zhang had never complained when every day she handed him such a miserly sum that he would barely be able to afford to drink tea with his friends. Over the years the money Zhang made from his cat paintings had ensured that he and his friends were able to enjoy far more cheering beverages than tea.

Zhang's passing was mourned by his many admirers. He was rightly regarded as one of the leading pioneers in the revitalization of Chinese calligraphy. In Beijing his extraordinary creative energy had inspired Huang Miaozi, Gu Gan, Han Yu and others to apply both their imagination and their painterly talents to giving this ancient art a modern appeal. As Zhang put it in his personal motto, borrowed from Shi Tao (1642–1710): 'The brush and ink should follow the times.'

LI LUOGONG

1917–91

The 'wild beast'

85 In 1973 Li was savagely criticized by Jiang Qing for his dramatic rendering of Mao's most personal poem, beginning 'I lost my proud poplar', which was about the death of his first wife.

In the late twentieth century few people did as much as Li Luogong to revitalize the art of calligraphy in China. This is perhaps slightly ironic, when one considers that he probably knew more about Western abstract art than any other Chinese artist of his generation. After years of thought and experimentation, he developed a fascinating new style, combining the pictograms that are at the root of the earliest Chinese calligraphy with the spirit of Western post-Impressionist painting.

From fauvism to modern calligraphy

Although born into a peasant family, Li managed to gain entry to the Shanghai Special College of Fine Arts, where, from 1936 to 1940, he studied the techniques of Western painting. After graduation – and despite the fact that China and Japan were then at war – Li decided to study post-Impressionism in Tokyo, since more was known about the subject there than in China. By the time he returned to China in 1944, he had developed a particular fondness for the group of French painters known as the Fauves (meaning 'wild beasts') and had modelled his own style closely on the work of the painter Maurice de Vlaminck (1876–1958).

After the Communist takeover in 1949, Li became head of the Fine Arts Department of a college in Tianjin. His heavy administrative duties left him little time to paint, which he did slowly at the best of times. In his free time he found it easier to settle down to enjoy the pleasures of seal carving. His interest in this art stemmed from his childhood in Fujian province, where he had grown up not far from Shoushan, a district whose stones are highly regarded by seal carvers.

In the 1950s one of Li's former teachers, Professor Liu Haisu, pressed him to create a new form of art that would combine the qualities of Chinese art with modern Western techniques. As Li would first need to understand fully the essence of Chinese art, Liu suggested that he begin by looking at early Chinese calligraphy: the script etched on the oracle bones used for divination, the inscriptions cast on early bronze ritual vessels or moulded on bricks and tiles, and finally the brushwork that had begun to emerge in the Qin and Han dynasties. With great foresight, Professor Liu predicted that this process would take some twenty years.

Li took up the challenge with enthusiasm. Indeed, he was obsessive about the development of his art. Sometimes he got so absorbed in what he was doing that he would work right through the night. On one such occasion his mother brought him breakfast in the belief that he had just got up. Still concentrating on his calligraphy, Li inadvertently dipped the dough stick she had given him into his ink instead of the soy sauce, took a bite, and then wondered why the sauce was so tasteless.

Li's hopes of quietly pursuing his study of calligraphy were shattered in 1957, when he was condemned as a 'Rightist'. The accusations about his foreign ways may well have been fuelled by the fact that he had chosen to live in Tokyo during a period in which Japan was engaged in a major war with China. He was so severely criticized that his wife came under great pressure from her colleagues and employers to divorce him. He was punished by being sent to endure hard labour in the countryside, where in winter he had to cut ice from the ponds so that it could be stored and then used to keep food fresh in the summer.

In 1960 Li was finally allowed to return to the university, although only as an assistant in the reference library, not as a teacher. Believing that he now had virtually no chance of ever being allowed to teach Western painting or to exhibit his works, he decided to concentrate on developing his calligraphy and seal carving. The latter was easier for him than the former. By this stage, Li had already carved thousands of seals. Towards the end of his life, when he was in his seventies, he claimed to have made a total of more than ten thousand.

Knowing that no one would publish the works of a 'Rightist', Li adopted the simple expedient of writing under another name, switching from his birth name of Li Limin to 'Li Luogong'. The literal meaning of his new name was 'the gentleman with the plodding stamina of a camel'. He meant it to symbolize the extent to which, regardless of hardship, he was prepared to plod on with the development of his art, just like a camel crossing the desert.

The first major occasion on which Li used his new name was when he published a book of his seal carvings in 1962. These works had a freshness about them that stemmed from his use of early pictographic forms of characters that were close to symbols. His favourite seal bore the two characters he had chosen to use as his artistic name – *Tuo Zong* ('in the steps of the camel') – which he felt reflected the suffering he had undergone. Not surprisingly, he was delighted, and greatly encouraged to develop his seal carving further, when Guo Moruo (pp. 80–90), China's leading cultural figure of the day, personally praised his work in 1963.

Details of fig. 86

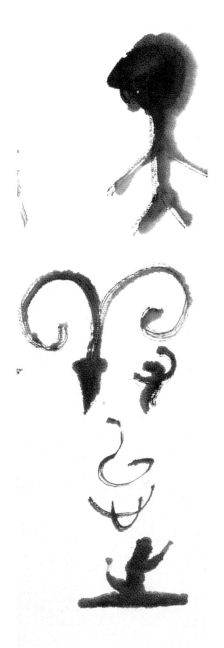

When the Cultural Revolution broke out in 1966, Li suffered even greater harassment and vilification than he had in 1957. Not only was he publicly condemned as 'a ghost and a monster', but he was physically maltreated and his possessions vandalized. Then, in the winter of 1969, he was banished from Tianjin, a city he loved, to Lingchuan, a county town in the south-western province of Guangxi. There he worked as a librarian in the local cultural bureau. His job was uninteresting and his living conditions disagreeable.

Li's new location was, however, not without its advantages. He appreciated the fact that he was near the city of Guilin, which lies amid some of the most beautiful scenery in China, where the Lijiang River flows through the plain dotted by the famous sugarloaf mountains. He also had time to think about art and began quietly trying his hand at creating a new form of calligraphy. Initially, he went back to the symbolic, pictographic style of early Chinese characters, whose forms were bold and dramatic.

Li's new calligraphy was innovative not only in the style of the characters he used, but also in its unusual brushwork. Although he was passionate about calligraphy, Li had never really mastered the traditional art of using a Chinese calligraphy brush, wherein the skill of the calligrapher is closely linked to his ability to manoeuvre the tip and middle of the brush. Like that of Western-style oil painters, Li's technique was based on using the side of a straight-edged brush. When he turned to calligraphy, he developed a new brush to suit his own taste and skills, by simply cutting the tip off a conventional Chinese one and applying the ink to the sides, rather than filling the brush with ink in the usual way. This new implement enabled Li to create brushstrokes in which the ink was concentrated on the outside, leaving the centre white.

A storm over tears

Despite his banishment to Guangxi, Li was still well remembered in Beijing for his seal carving. In 1972, when the authorities staged an exhibition of the Chinese works of art that were going to be sent to Tokyo to mark the restoration of diplomatic relations between the two countries, a collection of his seals was among the exhibits. Guo Moruo wrote a calligraphic inscription to accompany them.

Later the same year, Li was invited to submit one of his pieces of calligraphy for inclusion in an exhibition in Japan being organized by the China Council for the Promotion of International Trade. Fully aware that the innovative nature of his work and the boldness of his style would command attention, Li prudently decided that the content of his piece should be one

127

of Mao's poems. The one he chose began with the words 'I lost my proud poplar', its message being 'I know how you feel about losing your husband, as I lost my wife' (see fig. 44 on p. 51). Li loved this poem and had started working on calligraphic versions of it in the early 1960s, soon after it was first published.

The Guangxi authorities were happy to submit Li's piece to Beijing. As was then the custom, every person's work had to be vetted by the Ministry of Culture. Unfortunately for Li, the Ministry was then under the influence of Jiang Qing, Mao's third (and somewhat paranoid) wife. She hated this poem. This fact alone would have spurred her to condemn Li's piece, but her hatred of its content was matched by her distaste for the avant-garde style of his calligraphy. It was the style of one single character, however, that gave her an opening through which to get her claws into Li. In his poem Mao says that 'Tears of joy pour forth like mighty rain' at the thought of the two spouses finding peace in Heaven. When Li wrote the character *yu* for 'rain', he did so in an unusual way that made it seem as if the rain were a cascade of tears.

No portrayal of tears in Chinese calligraphy ever caused such a political storm. Jiang Qing immediately launched into a tirade, hysterically declaring that Li had been 'crying under Communism for twenty years'. In retrospect, one can see that this attack on Li's piece was actually part of Jiang's widening campaign of attacks on Premier Zhou Enlai, who was the leading moderate within the ruling elite of the Communist party. Nevertheless, the outlook for Li himself was bleak. As long as Jiang remained a power in the land, his works would never be included in national exhibitions, nor would he be considered for a good appointment. The only thing that saved him

86 Li's rendering of the classical poem *The Indomitable Soul* was, in effect, a statement about his own life.

was the fact that he lived in remote Guangxi and was greatly liked by several influential local people.

In the aftermath of this incident, Li rediscovered his copy of a poem by the Chinese ruler Cao Cao (155–220) entitled *The Indomitable Soul*. He felt that it reflected his own determination to persist in what he was doing in spite of the wrongs he had suffered. The words are stirring:

> *Although long lives the tortoise wise,*
> * in the end, he cannot but die.*
> *The dragon in the mist may rise,*
> * but in the dust he too shall lie.*
>
> *Although the stabled steed is old,*
> * he dreams to run a thousand li.*
> *In life's December, heroes bold*
> * indomitable still will be.*
>
> *It is not up to Heaven alone*
> * to lengthen or shorten our days.*
> *Let's cultivate our minds and live on*
> * through long years, if we know the ways.*

Li wrote this poem out many times. Most of his early versions measured about 30 × 150 cm. On the similarly sized piece in the British Museum (fig. 86), he added the words: 'How happy I feel at this thought! I croon this poem as I ought.'

After he had moved into more spacious accommodation in Guilin in 1978, Li was able to write out the poem on the scale he had always wished,

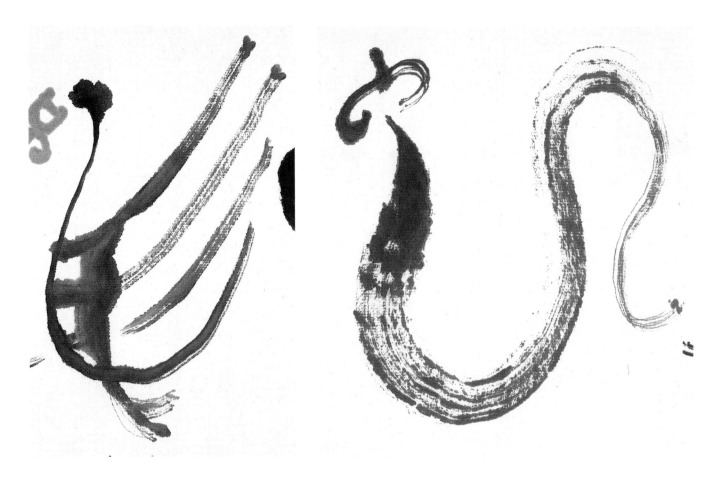

two metres high by six metres long. To reinforce his cheerful mood, he added a seal to the upper right-hand corner that read: 'My ambition is as lofty as the clouds.'

Details of fig. 86

Within three years of Jiang Qing's diatribe against Li, she and the other members of the Gang of Four had been overthrown. To mark the occasion, Li wrote a powerful piece consisting of just two characters: *Da Gui* ('Beat the Ghosts'). On the one hand, this is a play on the term 'ghosts and monsters', which was one of the worst accusations that could be made against anyone during the Cultural Revolution, and one that had been used against Li himself. On the other hand, opponents of the Gang of Four had regarded them as 'evil ghosts', and that was the term widely used to condemn them after their defeat.

Expressing feelings more openly

By 1978 the Chinese Communist Party was beginning to repair some of the damage that had been inflicted on people during the Cultural Revolution. For example, those who had not already returned home were now free to do so. Although Li could have returned to Tianjin, he and his wife decided to stay in Guangxi, as the authorities were now willing to provide them with an apartment that was not only much more comfortable but was within the city of Guilin itself. In the more relaxed atmosphere that now

prevailed in China, Li, like other artists, could express himself much more freely (see fig. 87 and detail). Stylistically he continued to experiment with his highly innovative approach to calligraphy, devoting much time and effort to ensuring that the form and composition of his characters evoked the feelings he wished to convey.

In the 1980s China's new leader Deng Xiaoping embarked on reforming the country and opening up its links with the outside world. Li's delight in these changes, and in Deng's recognition of the value of diversity, was reflected in several of his works and can be detected in the following lines:

> *Out there, in the great ocean,*
> *there are wonderful talents yet to be discovered.*

> *We cannot all follow the same rules.*
> *We must seek knowledge from others*
> *and forge ahead courageously.*

During the early part of the decade, Li encouraged Huang Miaozi and Gu Gan in their efforts to create their own form of Modernist art. Not surprisingly, Li was one of the main contributors to the ground-breaking exhibition of Modernist calligraphy held in Beijing in 1985. Thanks to his inspiration and teaching, the town of Guilin became, and has remained, a leading centre in China for Modernist and Avant-Garde calligraphers.

Throughout this period of change, Li remained grateful to the city of Guilin for the shelter it had afforded him in hard times, as well as welcoming the delights it now offered. A substantial proportion of all of the pieces he wrote are about Guilin. Perhaps his feelings are best summed up in the words he used in one of his late works:

> *One would rather be a resident of Guilin than an immortal.*

Li played an extremely important role in the development of modern Chinese calligraphy. In the late 1970s, after the death of Zhang Zhengyu, it was Li who gave the greatest impetus to the Modernist movement through the uncompromising boldness of his style. The 'wild beast' would have been delighted by the extent to which the great art of calligraphy developed in the years following his death.

87 In the late 1970s Li gave this piece of calligraphy (top picture, with detail below) to his old friend Gao Mang, a master of the Socialist Realism school of art who had studied in Moscow:

Time passes, tides ebb and flow,
But calligraphy and painting
will retain one's youth for ever
– as we know.

5 THE CLASSICISTS

SHA MENGHAI

1900–92

The gentlemanly scholar of 'Heaven on Earth'

88 Sha managed to survive the many campaigns mounted against intellectuals in the New China with less pain than most of his peers.

The Chinese have a saying that 'Above is heaven and below are Suzhou and Hangzhou'. Suzhou's charm lies in the beautiful gardens within the walls of its great houses, while the appeal of Hangzhou derives from the West Lake, surrounded by hills, cloaked in soft mists and set amidst a profusion of flowers and trees. It was in the idyllic setting of Hangzhou that Sha Menghai established his reputation as a distinguished calligrapher in the New China. To achieve this standing, he would be called upon to employ considerable political shrewdness in order to avoid misfortune.

From art to politics and back

Sha grew up near Ningbo, the main port of Zhejiang province, where his family had quite a large house. His father was a doctor of traditional medicine who took an interest in both calligraphy and seal carving. It was at the local school that Sha was introduced to the Chinese classics and developed his enthusiasm for the art of calligraphy.

In his mid-twenties Sha went to work in Shanghai as a tutor to a merchant's family. He was sufficiently talented as a calligrapher and seal carver to be taken on as a pupil by two of the greatest practitioners of the day. The first was the elderly Wu Changshuo (1844–1927), the leading artist of his time. Since Sha had long been attracted to the daring boldness of Wu's calligraphy and seal carving, he was delighted to be taught by him. The second was Kang Youwei (1858–1927), the great mandarin who had tried and failed to reform the Qing dynasty at the turn of the century. In his retirement Kang gained a reputation for the firmness and inner strength of his calligraphy, as well as for his ability to write large characters that were not simply decorative but had real 'personality'.

Sha was lucky not only with his calligraphy teachers, but also with his political connections. Because he was from Ningbo, it was not difficult for him to meet senior people in the Nationalist Party. President Jiang Jieshi (Chiang Kaishek) himself came from that district and preferred to employ people who spoke his own dialect. Through these connections Sha was introduced to Zhu Jiahua, the Minister of Education, who had formerly been the head of Beijing University and was a good scholar of the Chinese classics and a connoisseur of antiquities. Zhu was so taken with this personable

133

young man with his excellent calligraphy that he took him on as his private secretary. Over the next few years he provided Sha with a remarkable, albeit informal, education.

In 1938, as the Japanese stepped up their military onslaught against China, the Nationalist Government moved its capital to Chongqing, some 2,500 kilometres up the Yangzi River. Sha went too, and after a short period in Chongqing was promoted to President Jiang Jieshi's secretariat. After the war, Sha was put in charge of tracing the genealogy of the Jiang family, which brought him into direct and regular contact with Jiang himself for the first time.

From the very beginning of his career, Sha was admired for his calligraphy. He used regular script both when writing official papers in the secretariat and when writing for pleasure. He wrote slightly broad, though beautifully balanced characters, which had a certain pertness about them. Professor Liu Zengfu (pp. 203–9) once pointed out to me that 'His work is that of a cultivated gentleman. The strokes are thick, smooth and clear, so that the characters have a weight that makes them sit comfortably on the page, while having the bright clarity of an autumn day.'

Sha was more aware than many in the Nationalist Party that the days of the old regime were numbered. As early as the 1920s, his three brothers had joined the Communist Party in the belief that it, and not the Nationalist Party, would be able to bring social justice to China. Sha himself had sided with the Nationalists, on the grounds that at least one member of the family should have a foot in the other camp, just in case things did not work out as they hoped. By 1948 his brothers were well established in the Communist Party hierarchy. As the Communist armies advanced on Shanghai in 1949 and Jiang Jieshi prepared to flee to Taiwan, Sha's brothers urged him to stay in China, arguing that he would have nothing to fear under the new regime. Having received similar assurances from Guo Moruo (pp. 80–90), the leading scholar of the Communist Party whom he had known in Chongqing, Sha accepted their advice.

He soon returned to his native Zhejiang, where one of his brothers, Sha Wenhan, had been appointed as the first Communist governor of the province. In 1954 Sha was made director of the history department at the newly established Zhejiang Museum in Hangzhou, the provincial capital.

As well as enjoying a growing reputation as a calligrapher who wrote beautiful regular script, Sha had already displayed a flair for writing big characters. In 1955 he was given his first real chance to demonstrate this talent when he was invited to write the name plaque for the Da Xiong Bao Dian pavilion at Hangzhou's famous Lingyin Temple (see fig. 38 on p. 45).

Detail of fig. 89

It was probably the grandest and most prestigious public commission in China at that time.

Sha rose to the occasion. He tied together the three largest brushes he could find and set to work on enormous sheets of paper spread out on the floor. The harmonious vigour of his four huge characters, each of which was three metres square, was much acclaimed. He did not, however, enjoy the experience, which he said made him feel like 'an ox ploughing a field'.

A great survivor

Besides being skilled with a brush, Sha was also politically shrewd. He kept his opinions to himself and his emotions firmly under control. He never expressed views on political issues and always sought to mollify anyone who made requests of him. This approach brought its rewards. When his brother Sha Wenhan was condemned as a 'Rightist' and lost his post as governor in 1958, Sha was left unscathed, despite his earlier close connections with Jiang Jieshi. The worst thing that happened to him during the late 1950s was the removal of his signature from the name plaque of the Da Xiong Bao Dian pavilion. When Premier Zhou Enlai learned of this during a visit to the temple in 1960, he said that since it was Sha's brother who was the 'Rightist', not Sha, the signature should be restored. And so it was.

Having thus been exonerated by the premier, Sha began to receive public commissions once again. That same year he created the name plaque for the Tian Wang Dian, one of the main pavilions at the Longhua Temple in Shanghai. Three years later, in 1963, he was appointed a professor at the Zhejiang Academy of Fine Arts (now the China National Academy of Fine Arts). Shortly afterwards, when he was commissioned to produce a four-metre-wide rendering of Mao's poem *Beidaihe*, he felt that his former political problems were firmly behind him.

At the Academy, Sha settled down to concentrate on calligraphy and write books on its history and aesthetics. His archaeological and epigraphical studies influenced the style of his later years. He began to study more closely the works of two famous calligraphers: Yan Zhenqing (709–785), famed for the clarity of his regular script, and Wang Xianzhi (344–386), whom Sha admired for the freshness of his running script, in which the strokes within each character, and often between characters, were boldly linked together.

Analysing the way in which Sha's calligraphy evolved over the years, one can begin to see more clearly the two different strands that ran through his personality. Outwardly he was a self-effacing man, overly polite in his efforts to avoid making enemies. Throughout his life he preserved a delicacy of brushwork in his calligraphy that reflected this genuinely gentle side of his character. This trait, however, is evenly balanced by a simple and forceful style of brushwork conveying a strong impression of emotion, inner strength and determination.

Despite the fact that Sha's calligraphy became increasingly bold as he matured, he remained notably cautious about the content of his works. He wrote few poems, preferring to use poetry by others that was politically uncontroversial. Often he confined himself to writing moralistic maxims, such as 'Strive' (*Fenfa*).

When the Cultural Revolution erupted in Hangzhou, the Red Guards were particularly savage with those scholars who were in prominent university positions or had expressed 'reactionary' views. Sha was fortunate in that he was not the head of the Academy or the Museum and had been careful not to voice any political views in the course of his work.

Sha suffered nonetheless. His house was ransacked by the Red Guards and his youngest daughter denounced him as a 'counter-revolutionary' because of his earlier links with Jiang Jieshi. This led to his being 'detained for investigation' for two years and forced to work as a sweeper. His signature was again removed from the name plaque on the Da Xiong Bao Dian pavilion at the Lingyin Temple, although his calligraphy remained in place, mainly because the army had been sent in to protect all the major museums and cultural sites from the rampaging destruction of the Red Guards.

By the standards of the time Sha was remarkably lucky, given the charges made against him. But worse was yet to come. After his release in 1971, his daughter died as a result of the maltreatment she herself had later suffered. Her death was a terrible blow to both Sha and his wife. The following year, Sha began to practise his calligraphy once more, partially as a means of comforting himself.

He was, of course, delighted by the overthrow of the Gang of Four in October 1976. That winter, he trudged through one of Hangzhou's rare snowstorms to see his old friend Liu Xin, to whom he remarked that he felt both he and his calligraphy had been given a new lease of life.

To mark the occasion, Sha gave his friend two scrolls on which he had written out poems by Mao Zedong. One described mountains 'like great waves surging in a crashing sea'. The other was *Reascending Jingkangshan*, a poem Mao had written in 1965 after revisiting the site of one of his early tortuous marches across mountains. It ends with the lines: 'We shall return amid triumphant song and laughter. Nothing is hard in this world, if you dare to scale the heights.' There was no risk involved in giving this poem to

Detail of fig. 89

Liu Xin. Although Sha had not scaled any heights, the words were an apt expression of his feelings in the aftermath of the Cultural Revolution.

By the time the Cultural Revolution had finished, Sha was in his mid-seventies. He welcomed the return to power of Deng Xiaoping and was in favour of his reformist economic policies. Sha was delighted to be appointed director of the Hangzhou Museum and also chairman of the Xi Ling Seal-Carving Society when it was reopened in 1979, marking the seventy-fifth anniversary of its foundation. He was especially proud of this second post, as the Society had been founded by Wu Changshuo, his former teacher, who had given him a scroll praising his skills as a seal carver.

With the establishment of the Chinese Calligraphers' Association in 1981 and his appointment as a vice-chairman, Sha suddenly became a national figure. He was now able to settle down to being one of the grand old men of Chinese calligraphy, which for him was like a dream come true. From then on until his death in 1992, there was a continuous demand for his calligraphy for both cultural and commercial use. In Hangzhou a great deal of his work can still be seen, including the name plaque for the city's most beautiful feature, the Su Causeway (*Su Di*), constructed by the eleventh-century poet-administrator Su Dongpo. In his mid-eighties Sha rewrote the huge name plaque for the Da Xiong Bao Dian pavilion at the Lingyin Temple. He also produced name plaques for scores of shops, hotels and restaurants. Probably no other artist has left his mark so visibly on a Chinese city.

Sha's vice-chairmanship of the Chinese Calligraphers' Association won him commissions from far afield. In Beijing he created a large calligraphic piece for display in the Great Hall of the People and an inscription for the art shop Rong Bao Zhai (which already had one by his old friend Guo Moruo). In Shanghai he was asked to provide the name plaque for a museum that had been established in the house where his friend Shen Yinmo had lived from 1945 until his death in 1971. In Shaoxing, not far from his home town, Sha was responsible for the plaque on the memorial temple of Wang Xizhi (303–361), who wrote the *Orchid Pavilion Preface*, a work many people regard as the finest piece of calligraphy ever written. In addition, numerous inscriptions that Sha wrote have been carved into cliffs and rocks at scenic sites across the country.

Sha hoped that his honourable behaviour and high reputation as a calligrapher and scholar would lead to his appointment to the Chinese People's Political Consultative Conference. In this aspiration, however, he was disappointed. It was an honour reserved largely for those who had genuinely suffered during the Cultural Revolution – and on that score there were numerous talented scholars far better qualified than himself.

A late flowering

Chinese connoisseurs of calligraphy often express the feeling that Sha's work lacks the 'inner spiritual quality' that is so highly prized in traditional calligraphy. Nevertheless, it is widely agreed that the work he produced in his eighties, at a time when the political climate in China was more relaxed than it had been since 1949, displays an alluring fluidity and brilliance of technique. His strength was impressive. At the age of eighty-seven he was still able to write out a four-metre-square version of the character for 'dragon' (*long*). Even in his nineties, just before his death, Sha's hand never trembled and his brushwork remained smooth.

It was during these later years that Sha wrote out one of his finest poems (fig. 89):

> *Red apricot blossom and pink butterflies*
> > *can be seen over the wall,*
> *While outside the window, there are green willows*
> > *and yellow orioles.*
>
> *To best enjoy the spring breezes,*
> > *join those who walk along Su Dongpo's causeway*
> > *across the West Lake.*

The juxtaposition of the soft green trailing willow and the intensely bright blossoms beautifully captures the great charm of the blossoming of spring in Hangzhou. One of the best ways to experience that pleasure is indeed to walk along the Su Causeway, with the lake shimmering on either side of it and misty hills and temples rising in the distance.

Sha died in 1992 at the age of ninety-two. For some people, his death on the tenth day of the tenth month – the date on which the Republic of China in Taiwan celebrates its national day – was an unfortunate reminder of his previous links with the Nationalist Party and with Jiang Jieshi himself. But those who also knew that he had died at precisely ten minutes past ten in the morning felt that the coincidence of the four tens, which the Chinese regard as being so auspicious, was yet another indication of how lucky Sha had been during his life.

Sha may not have received the political rewards he would have liked, but he did enjoy many happy years in Hangzhou. Before his death, he also had the immense satisfaction of knowing that in his home town of Ningbo the authorities had begun constructing 'The Sha Menghai Academy of Calligraphy' to commemorate his achievements and perpetuate the study of the art he so revered.

89 This poem is a delightful evocation of the view Sha enjoyed both from the museum and from the grounds of the Xi Ling Seal-Carving Society, where he spent many of his happiest moments.

聖善堂前粉堞環橋

寰外黄鸝日慶墨風

寂寞湯頭人在蘇堤

沙孟海

LIN SANZHI

1898–1989

The man with the 'iron line'

When Guo Moruo first saw Lin Sanzhi's calligraphy in 1972, he declared it the best that had been written in China for three centuries. Lin, already seventy-four years of age, became famous overnight.

Poetry and martial arts

Lin was born into a peasant family living near Caishiji, a village located some fifty kilometres south of Nanjing in Anhui province. The great Tang poet Li Bai had spent the last years of his life in Caishiji – a fact that had an enduring effect on the quality of local education. Despite his family's poor financial situation, Lin therefore received quite a good classical education. In addition, the local enthusiasm for Li Bai generated in him a passion for poetry that he was to maintain throughout his life.

By the age of twelve Lin was writing the couplets on red paper that his neighbours customarily hung on either side of their doors to celebrate the Chinese New Year. His real passion, however, was painting. By his twenties, he had become good enough to make a living from selling his works.

Despite this promising start, Lin knew that he still had much to learn. In 1929, at the age of thirty-two, he moved to Shanghai, where he eked out a living while at the same time taking lessons from Huang Binhong (1864–1955), a famous landscape painter from his home province of Anhui. After two years, however, Lin was so impoverished that he was forced to rejoin his wife and young son in his home town and take up work as a school-teacher. Nevertheless, in the ensuing years he followed Huang's advice and travelled extensively to scenic places to make on-the-spot sketches, a practice that endowed his paintings with a distinctive vitality.

In addition to painting, Lin took a keen interest in Buddhism, the most popular faith in China at the time. He also practised the martial arts, which he had first taken up as a young man to improve his fitness. There was a link between these two interests in that some of the Buddhist monks of the Zen (Chan) sect believed mastery of the martial arts to be a more valuable aid to meditation than the study of classical texts. After visiting the Shaolin monastery in Henan province, whose monks are renowned for their martial arts prowess and extraordinary willpower, Lin felt that his own physical and spiritual strength had been greatly enhanced.

90 Having studied martial arts in his youth, Lin had an iron will and great physical strength, even into his old age.

RIGHT: Detail of fig. 91

In 1947 Lin's growing reputation as a painter and poet led to the offer of a professorship of art and literature at the university in Hefei, the capital of Anhui province. He declined, apparently preferring in those troubled days to stay close to Nanjing, which was then the seat of the Nationalist Government of Jiang Jieshi (Chiang Kaishek). His reluctance to move was compounded by his wife's refusal to leave their family home.

After the Communist takeover in 1949, Lin became a minor government official in Jiangpu, even though he was not a member of the Party. By 1956 he had been made deputy mayor. When Jiangpu was incorporated into Nanjing in 1958, Lin was appointed to the Standing Committee of the city's Political Consultative Conference – a position involving only a modicum of work and carrying only a small salary, but one that bestowed considerable status. When he retired a year later at the age of sixty, he once again turned to art. In 1963 he became a teacher at the Jiangsu Academy of Chinese Painting in Nanjing. Much as Lin loved landscape painting, he began to devote an increasing amount of his time to mastering the fast-flowing cursive style of calligraphy, which he believed best expressed both his skill and his spirit.

At this stage in his life, however, Lin was better known as a poet than as a calligrapher. Indeed, when his works started to be published in the milder political atmosphere of the 1980s, it became clear that he probably ranked among the finest poets in modern China.

Lin's poems provide a fascinating insight into his attitudes about life and about China before the Cultural Revolution. In them he expressed himself in a plain, classical style similar to that used during the Song dynasty. Even late in his life, his poems still had the freshness and openness of a bright, youthful spirit. They were inspired by the ordinary events of his life, his relationships with his friends, the changes in the seasons, his travels and his visits to the great scenic spots in China. Many of his poems were also humorous and self-mocking.

Tragedy and transformation

Lin was known almost as much for his rustic simplicity as for his intellect. Although his art and poetry were extremely sophisticated, he thoroughly enjoyed the everyday things in life, living modestly and spending much of his time with ordinary people. Some of his closest friends were monks or hermits, who shared his taste for solitude as well as for basic country food. Lin never made any effort to hide his emotions. When he first saw the film version of the popular novel *A Dream of Red Mansions* in the 1960s, he was so moved that he burst into tears – the only person in the audience to do so.

In the 1950s and early 1960s Lin believed that socialism would bring better times for China. It was an optimism that made the trauma of the Cultural Revolution all the greater for him. At the outset, the Red Guards destroyed many of his favourite objects and persecuted him, primarily because of his fervent belief in the importance of Chinese culture and his unwillingness to confess to 'crimes' he had not committed. His misery at this situation was soon compounded by the death of his wife.

After her funeral, Lin slipped quietly out of Nanjing. Everyone seemed to assume that he had died of grief, and amid the turmoil they soon forgot about him. In fact, over the next three years he lived first in Yangzhou and then in Wujiang, both of them places where he felt more secure. During this time he kept depression at bay by discreetly teaching a small, committed group of young calligraphers, one of whom was Wang Dongling (pp. 163–71). To safeguard his students, should any outsiders take too close an interest in what they were doing, Lin took most of the texts he asked them to write out in their exercises from Mao's own poems or prose.

In 1969 Lin decided that it was safe to return to his family village of Caishiji to live with his son. His increasing deafness had heightened his sense of isolation and compounded his depression over the implications of the Cultural Revolution for China's future. Once again, he struggled to achieve peace of mind through the regular practice of calligraphy.

Lin's life was soon to be transformed yet again by a terrible accident. During a visit to a Chinese bathhouse in 1970 he stumbled and inadvertently plunged his right hand into boiling water. It was so badly burned that three of his fingers became fused together. Although Lin knew that an operation would be excruciatingly painful, he insisted that the hospital separate his fingers so that he could write again.

After his wounds had healed, his brushwork was no longer elegant and fluid, but exhibited a certain rawness and naïvety. Before long these qualities hardened into the so-called 'iron line' that became the defining feature of his work in his later years. With long, thin, hard brushstrokes, often executed with a dryish brush, he formed individual characters and strings of characters that were taut with energy, reflecting the inner strength of a man who had survived only as a result of his iron determination.

A new dawn

To mark the re-establishment of diplomatic relations with Japan in 1972, Premier Zhou Enlai agreed to Guo Moruo's suggestion that the magazine *People's China* should publish a special edition featuring the work of modern Chinese calligraphers. Lin's old friend Tian Yuan, the editor of the *New*

91 Lin's rendering of Du Mu's poem *Going up the Hill*:

A slanting, stony path rises far up the chilly hill
To where men live amidst the fleecy clouds.
I stop my carriage to admire the maple grove at dusk,
Whose frozen leaves are redder than the flowers of early spring.

RIGHT: Detail

142

China Daily, arranged for one of Lin's pieces to be submitted to the selection committee, which was chaired by Guo.

The committee was deeply moved by Lin's contribution. When the scroll was hung up for inspection, Qi Gong (pp. 146–52) took one look at Lin's unique and novel 'iron line' script, then stood in front of it and bowed three times as a mark of respect. Guo was so impressed by Lin's calligraphy that he proclaimed him China's best calligrapher of the past 300 years. He insisted that the first piece to be illustrated in the magazine should be Lin's, and not his own as originally planned.

It was widely agreed that Lin's work was exceptional, although many of the cognoscenti felt that perhaps Guo had been so delighted to see fine calligraphy again that he had been over-lavish in his praise. However, there was little objection to this, since through his tribute Guo rendered calligraphy once again respectable as an art form.

The impact of Lin's piece was all the greater because he had shrewdly chosen as his text Mao's much-loved poem *Huichang*, written in 1935 (see p. 107). It begins with the words 'A new dawn breaks in the East' (*Dong fang yu xiao*). This aptly captured the mood of China's moderates, who yearned for a 'new dawn' after the ordeal of the Cultural Revolution.

The illustration of Lin's piece and Guo's effusive praise of it even excited interest in Japan. When a delegation of Japanese calligraphers visited Nanjing in 1973 they made a specific request to meet Lin. The local authorities, who were not yet aware of Lin's newly acquired status, had to send a car to fetch him from Wujiang. The Japanese were especially fascinated by Lin's calligraphy because it seemed to them to possess certain Japanese qualities. This may reflect Lin's training as a painter and the fact that he tended to compose his calligraphy in the painterly way of the Japanese. He also used his ink in the very dry manner generally favoured in Japan. Indeed, it is possible that he had based some of his stylistic elements on the Japanese calligraphy he had seen in the 1920s and 1930s. Whatever the reason, Lin suddenly became quite famous.

Although other artists would have relished the sort of accolades that were being heaped upon Lin by both his Chinese and his Japanese admirers, he showed no sign of enjoying his new-found fame. He was very pleased, however, when the authorities arranged for him to return to Nanjing in 1973, well before many other victims of the Cultural Revolution were able to return to their old homes. Lin's fame also led him to become more prolific and to perform for a much wider audience. Fortunately, his flair for poetry complemented his calligraphy beautifully, imparting a special freshness to his work. Moreover, he wrote poetry with such great clarity that even people who normally had difficulty in understanding classical poems could often enjoy the ones that he had written.

Back in Nanjing, Lin resumed teaching on an informal basis. One of the calligraphers who returned to study under him was Wang Dongling. Although Lin was now something of a national figure, his personality had not changed. Just as before, he was totally straightforward in his dealings with his protégés, praising them for what he considered to be their achievements and chastising them for their shortcomings. Besides teaching, Lin also wrote essays about calligraphy.

As a result of his fame, many people were eager to own a piece of Lin's calligraphy. One of them was a man he referred to as Comrade Dong Yang, who in 1975 asked Lin to write out for him the poem *Going up the Hill* by Du Mu (803–852). Lin did so in his 'iron line' (fig. 91), which well suited the content of the poem. Since the last line reads 'whose frozen leaves are redder than the flowers of early spring', it is quite likely that Dong Yang chose this poem as a reflection of his own feelings about the Cultural Revolution. Its theme is similar to that of *The Red Leaves of the Western Hills*, written at the start of the Cultural Revolution by Marshal Chen Yi (pp. 91–9). In his poem Chen Yi compares true Communists to those leaves which reveal their finest colour in the harshest conditions.

Lin was, of course, extremely pleased when he learned of the fall of the Gang of Four in October 1976. One of the ways in which he celebrated it was by writing an allegorical poem on a picture a friend of his had painted of four crabs. Since crabs do not move in the same straightforward way as most creatures, it was an excellent way of alluding to the Gang of Four. But the emotional scars Lin bore from the Cultural Revolution could not be dealt with so lightly. A little later he wrote a poem about the suffering he had endured, adding that, despite everything, he still loved his country.

However, Lin soon felt able to focus on the more positive aspects of life and once again he wrote many poems and essays on poetry. In 1978 he was delighted, at the age of eighty-one, to be appointed to the Chinese People's Political Consultative Conference (along with his new friend and admirer Qi Gong). When he met Deng Xiaoping there for the first time, he could not contain his admiration for this man who he felt had done so much to bring China back on to the right course. Lin stretched out his arm and, with his thumb raised, declared loudly, 'You're great!'

The Japanese continued to pay homage to Lin. Many leading Japanese calligraphers travelled to Nanjing to honour the man they saw as the 'sage of cursive script'. Their numbers increased in 1988, when, as a conciliatory gesture to coincide with the fiftieth anniversary of the destruction of

144

92 One of Lin's last poems:
Comprehend and meditate on Buddha through the moonlight on the ground. Living here in my citadel of books, I am happy in my seclusion.

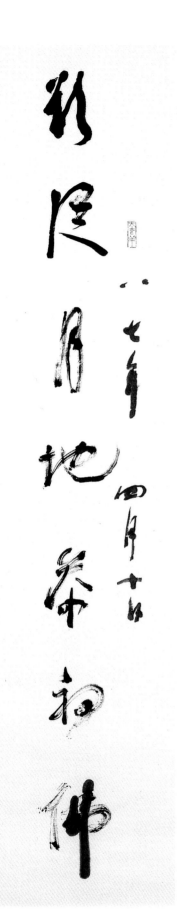

Nanjing, the Japanese Government sponsored an exhibition of Japanese calligraphy in the city – the largest such exhibition ever to have been staged in China up to that date.

Living out his old age at a time when the people of China were again free to worship openly, Lin composed several pieces on Buddhist themes. The poem illustrated in fig. 92, which he wrote in 1988 at the age of ninety, seems to refer to the role his Buddhist faith had played in sustaining him through the difficult years of the Cultural Revolution. It also reflects the fact that because of his deafness he spent more of his time in contemplation or reading the books that made up his extensive library.

To be close to Li Bai

In the period leading up to his death, Lin's thoughts were not only about Buddha. He often returned to visit Caishiji, where he had grown up and where his favourite poet, Li Bai, had spent his own last years. Lin told his friends that, after his death, he would like to be near Li Bai.

In 1989, when he was ninety-one years old, Lin wrote out the four characters *Sheng tian cheng fo* ('Fly to Heaven and become a Buddha'). This was to be his last calligraphic statement, as he died two days later. His death provoked a moment of national sadness. Newspapers carried lengthy obituaries and Lin was accorded a grand funeral. As he had wished, he was buried at Dangtu, not far from the tomb of Li Bai.

In 1990 the provincial government of Anhui decided to establish a museum of Lin's works close to the ancient Li Bai Memorial Hall at Caishiji. He was the first calligrapher to be honoured in this way in modern China. The importance attached to the event is evidenced by the fact that Lin's friend Qi Gong was asked to write the characters for the museum's name board and President Jiang Zemin agreed to perform the opening ceremony. The local authorities highlighted Jiang's patronage by placing in the surrounding park a sign pointing the way to the museum, on which the characters are copied from ones written by him. But in case visitors should fail to recognize Jiang's calligraphy, the sign carries his signature in letters almost as large as the inscription itself.

Lin's 'iron line' calligraphy and the Japanese interest it aroused greatly enhanced his reputation and influence, while Guo Moruo's acknowledgement of the quality of his Classical style was instrumental in re-establishing calligraphy as a prominent art form in China. In addition, the enduring freshness of his output encouraged other calligraphers to explore new styles. Lin can therefore be seen as having made an important contribution towards the emergence of China's Modernist school of calligraphy.

QI GONG

1912–

China's best-known living calligrapher

93 Qi Gong is highly renowned as a scholar and calligrapher. His charm and wit have further widened his circle of admirers. Here he is seen in his apartment in 1996 accompanied by the author – and clutching his favourite 'Ninja Turtle'.

Qi Gong is an unashamedly enthusiastic champion of the revitalization of traditional Chinese calligraphy. While others explore radical new approaches, his more traditional works continue to enjoy great popularity. But their appeal does not lie simply in the desire for continuity in a changing world. His calligraphy is imbued with a seemingly effortless elegance, achieved through skilful interplay between the proportions of his characters, which makes them both harmonious and lively.

From imperial to proletarian

Qi Gong's conservative credentials are impeccable. He is descended from Prince He, who was a brother of the Qian Long emperor (1736–95). After his father's early death, Qi Gong was brought up by his grandfather, a member of the Hanlin Academy which trained top mandarins and provided the imperial tutors. Following the death of his grandfather a few years later, when Qi Gong was only eleven years old, he was taken into the care of a maiden aunt who had become head of the family, whom Qi Gong always addressed by the Manchu word for 'uncle'.

Although Qi Gong never studied at a university, he did receive a fine classical education, as befits a member of the imperial household. From his early childhood he was taught the classics and calligraphy. One of his teachers was Prince Pu Ru (1896–1963), a brother of the last emperor, who lived in the splendid courtyarded palace in Beijing known as Gong Wang Fu (or the Mansion of Prince Gong, now open to the public).

During the 1930s Qi Gong began lecturing in classical Chinese at the Catholic Furen University in Beijing, which had moved into Gong Wang Fu. In academic circles he was considered to be one of the brightest young classicists of his generation and a talented connoisseur of antiquities. He was also recognized as possessing a distinct flair for poetry. After the Communist takeover in 1949, Furen University was merged with Beijing Normal University, where Qi Gong has been a professor ever since. One of the seals he carved in the early 1950s summed up his attitude towards life: 'Enjoy the entertainment, but don't forget your goal' (*Wan wu er bu sang zhi*).

In view of his background and the subject he was teaching, there was a fairly high risk that Qi Gong would fall victim to some political campaign during the early years of the Communist regime. He managed, however, to stay out of trouble until the 'Hundred Flowers Movement'. In 1956 he spoke out about painting – his hobby and a subject about which he felt passionately – in support of a plea for artists to be better paid that had been made by his friend Ye Gongchuo (pp. 74–9), a leading expert on Chinese culture and one of Mao Zedong's cultural companions.

In the vicious clampdown that followed this period of openness, even this modest request led to Qi Gong being denounced as a 'Rightist'. However, as he had done little more than voice his support, the stigma was soon lifted and he was able to resume teaching at the university and serving on the State Commission for Museums and Archaeology.

When the Cultural Revolution began in 1966, Qi Gong's background put him at greater risk. The atmosphere at Beijing University was tense. Indeed, many of the students travelled hundreds of kilometres to Qufu in Shandong province that October in order to destroy more than a thousand stone stelae in the mansion and graveyard of the descendants of Confucius. Qi Gong was criticized for his 'improper' attitudes, had his house ransacked by the Red Guards, and was made to clean toilets for a year and a half.

He could have fared much worse. Much to his surprise, it was his skill as an amateur calligrapher that helped protect him from more violent abuse. Fortunately, the revolutionaries who had seized control of the university were quick to realize that Qi Gong could promote their cause by writing out their revolutionary sentiments in his fine imperial script, which looked far more authoritative than anything they could produce.

Qi Gong then had another lucky break. In 1971 he contracted Ménière's disease just before he was due to be packed off to a 'cadre school' in the countryside, where university staff and students were being sent to 'improve themselves' by toiling alongside the peasants. This condition caused him to suffer a severe loss of balance, and consequently he was left behind. When he recovered, he found that no one seemed to care about him any more. The amusing account he wrote of his illness probably represents the only instance of the term 'Ménière's disease' ever making its way into poetry.

Thanks to his poor health and good fortune, Qi Gong now had time to work on improving his calligraphy. His interest in the art seems to have increased as a result of his recent 'revolutionary' experiences. He now started to study closely the work of two calligraphers renowned for their regular script: Ouyang Xun (557–641) and Liu Gongquan (778–865). He admired the former for his mastery of structure and balance, and the latter for his ability to convey power through slender strokes.

Although Qi Gong had been forgotten by most of his erstwhile tormentors, he was still well remembered by his admirers. Among them was Guo Moruo (pp. 80–90), one of the few leading cultural figures to have remained in office after the start of the Cultural Revolution. In 1972, when Guo was arranging for works by contemporary calligraphers to be published in a special edition of *People's China* to celebrate the restoration of diplomatic relations with Japan, he asked Qi Gong to sit on the selection panel.

The convening of the panel was an important occasion, as this was the first time since the Cultural Revolution began that artistic calligraphy had been given such prominence. It was at the selection meeting that Qi Gong first saw the work of Lin Sanzhi (pp. 140–5), a man who had seemingly emerged from nowhere and was to have a profound influence on Chinese calligraphy during the 1970s and 1980s.

Unlike some other leading calligraphers and painters, Qi Gong did not fall foul of Mao's neurotic wife, Jiang Qing, during the final years of the Cultural Revolution. Nevertheless, he shared the almost universal feeling of relief at the overthrow of the Gang of Four in 1976. In the months that followed, he and his friends often privately exchanged erudite poems as a way of either satirizing Jiang Qing and her fellow conspirators or venting their hatred of them. Interestingly, Qi Gong did not produce any calligraphy specifically commemorating the event. He felt that 'not having been brave enough to strike at the beasts when they were living, it would have been undignified to do so now that they were dead'.

Becoming well known

Just after the end of the Cultural Revolution, Qi Gong reached the age of sixty-five and formally retired from his post at the university. He continued to supervise graduate students, but now devoted even more attention to his calligraphy. The style he liked most was running script, and this led him to study the techniques of Dong Qichang (1555–1636) and Mi Fu

94 In 1984 Qi Gong created this pair of scrolls for one of the old revolutionaries in Guangzhou. His couplet can be translated as follows:

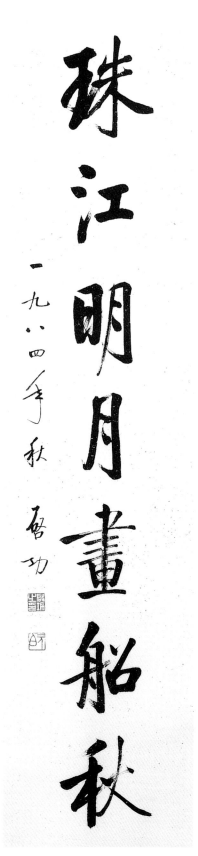

(1051–1107). Dong is best known for the slim elegance of his characters, which are often linked together in a rhythmic way, and Mi Fu for his effective combinations of light and thick strokes.

By training and temperament, Qi Gong had no desire to overstep the bounds of traditional calligraphy. He did, however, wish to give it a freshness and liveliness that would reflect his own character. The more he studied the works of earlier masters, the more he felt that more satisfying results could be achieved by moving away from the accepted practice of positioning characters in an imaginary box divided into 3×3 units. He developed a formula of 13×13 units, in which the key ratio was $5:3:5$ (see fig. 20 on p. 28). This made it possible to focus the core of the character on a smaller box in the middle of the frame and allowed more space for the longer vertical and diagonal strokes. Qi Gong's system has a marked effect on the balance and tensions within a character, as can be seen from fig. 94.

By using this approach, Qi Gong achieved exactly the freshness and liveliness that he had been seeking. His success was further enhanced by the skill with which he spaced his characters on the paper and by the complex visual rhythms he created by using heavy and light strokes – not just for individual characters, but also for the constituent elements within them. At times, the fine brushwork with which he executed the more complex parts of a character was exquisite.

The two scrolls illustrated here provide an excellent example of Qi Gong's calligraphy in his new style. They also reveal the subtlety of his poetry. In this couplet written for Ou Chu, one of the old revolutionaries in Guangzhou, Qi Gong mentions their respective homes in Beijing and Guangzhou. In the first line, about Beijing, he refers to the clouds of sunset touching the distant solitary stupa that stands on the island (Jasper Island) in Beihai Park. The second line is about the bright moon casting an autumnal light over the painted boats on the Pearl River which flows through Guangzhou. For the Chinese reader there is much ambiguity in these phrases, and a touch of humour as well.

The huge white stupa mentioned by Qi Gong is part of the Temple of Everlasting Peace that was built to celebrate the visit of the Dalai Lama to Beijing in 1651. It is not only one of Beijing's most beautifully austere landmarks, but is regarded by most Chinese as one of China's enduring symbols of imperial power. In the line about the Pearl River, the 'bright moon' is the moon of the mid-autumn festival, an occasion on which Chinese people traditionally enjoy themselves. The mention of the 'painted boats' of Guangzhou reinforces this message, as they have always been associated with pleasure, and especially that of a sensual nature.

The images juxtaposed in the couplet are so different as to raise the question of what point Qi Gong was trying to make. Certainly, after Deng Xiaoping authorized experimental economic reform in Guangdong in the early 1980s, life there became much less tense than in Beijing. Even so, the wording is a little risqué for the time. There are, however, many other possible readings of this couplet.

Although the elements of each character in it are carefully interwoven, Qi Gong, unlike other masters of running script, rarely links his characters with brushstrokes. Even when the rhythm of the brushwork gives the impression that characters are linked together, Qi Gong likes to let each of them have its own space. This is one of the reasons why he frequently writes couplets on specially prepared sheets of paper that have been decorated with a number of medallions matching the number of characters in each line. Regardless of the paper he uses, however, Qi Gong rarely writes large characters. Nor does he often date his work or add dedications, as he feels that these additions would impair the balance and appearance of his compositions.

Qi Gong's new style was already well developed when, in 1981, Deng Xiaoping agreed to the establishment, for the first time ever, of a Chinese Calligraphers' Association. Qi Gong was appointed as one of the vice-chairmen. His knowledge of the classics and calligraphy, as well as his family history, seemed to convey a sense of continuity and the reassertion of traditional values. Because Qi Gong was naturally deferential (as so many members of distinguished Manchu families tended to be), the authorities were fairly confident that he would not be troublesome. A few years later, they pressed him to assume the chairmanship of the association. In the end he obliged with a dignified acceptance of the appointment.

Qi Gong took his responsibilities even more lightly than the authorities had perhaps hoped he might. Indeed, he showed very little interest in directing the organization at all. When visitors asked him whether he was pleased to have been made chairman of the Chinese Calligraphers' Association, he would reply, with a wry smile, 'Hard to say' (*Shuo buqing*). And when asked what he considered to be the main achievements of the association, he said that he simply did not know.

Despite his great enthusiasm for calligraphy, Qi Gong remained actively involved in the study of several other subjects. As well as being appointed deputy director of the Chinese Institute for Literary and Historical Research, in 1986 he became chairman of the National Cultural Relics Authentication Committee. The authorities recognized his good work in these various fields by making him a member of the Chinese People's Political Consultative

Conference in 1979, and then appointing him to its standing committee in 1983 and 1987.

Elegiac charm and wit

For many people the formal appeal of Qi Gong's calligraphy is enhanced by the sophistication of its content. He has the distinction of being the last surviving classical poet who is also a leading calligrapher. Although he sometimes selects quotes from the works of famous poets, about half of his calligraphy is based on his own compositions. A number of his poems are about the nature of beauty and the transience of emotions. Some of them contain social commentaries, but he never encroaches upon political matters. He is also renowned in Beijing for the elegance of his writing and the sharpness of his wit. Often the phrases he uses in his compositions are full of plays on words, and many of his works include passages taken from popular comic dialogues. Viewers of his pieces can frequently be heard chuckling or even guffawing with laughter – a response not traditionally associated with calligraphy.

Qi Gong remained a prolific calligrapher until he began to have serious problems with his eyesight in 1999, when he was eighty-seven years old. In addition to all his pieces for friends and acquaintances, he has provided inscriptions and name plaques for many cultural sites and institutions, as well as restaurants and shops, and has even designed commercial logos. In the capital he has done work for his own university, the Beijing University Hospital, the Beijing Printing Works, the Poly Group (a company belonging to the People's Liberation Army), several antique shops, and the main banqueting hall of the Grand Hotel. His inscriptions also grace dozens of monuments and cultural sites across the country, including the Lin Sanzhi Memorial Museum at Caishiji in Anhui province.

Some of these inscriptions were supplied free of charge, but in most cases he has been willing to oblige only for a fee of US$1,000 or more. The fee corresponds to the size of the inscription and the number of characters it contains. In general, these 'bespoke' commissions tend to be marked by a flatness of style that perhaps reflects a boredom with them which his courtesy would never allow him to betray.

Qi Gong's calligraphy is widely copied. In some cases this has been done as a traditional mark of respect; more frequently, however, his work is copied fraudulently in the hope of selling a copy as the genuine article. In China there are probably more copies and fakes of Qi Gong's works than of any other artist's. There are even a number of shop signs written in a script intended to emulate his distinctive style and bearing a fake signature.

But when asked whether a work that has been attributed to Qi Gong is genuine or not, he always refuses to comment.

Qi Gong has earned a good deal of money through the sale of his calligraphy in China and abroad. Most of his earnings have been donated to the Beijing Normal University and put into a trust fund that supports scholarly research in history and calligraphy. Unlike some of the younger, more commercially successful calligraphers, Qi Gong still lives in a modest apartment within the grounds of the university. Here he receives a constant flow of visitors, many of whom come to present him with copies of their latest publications.

The ambassador

Since the mid-1980s Qi Gong has, in effect, been China's ambassador for calligraphy. Whenever he has travelled abroad, the Chinese Government has arranged for him to do so in appropriate style, accompanied by an escort who acts as both interpreter and assistant.

During the 1980s and early 1990s he made several visits to Hong Kong, Taiwan, Singapore, Korea and Japan, the places where Chinese calligraphy is most admired. In 1996, at the age of eighty-five, he finally made his great 'journey to the West', which was paid for by one of his many admirers then living in Hong Kong. Together with his friends Wang Shixiang and Fu Xinian, who were themselves well-known scholars of the Chinese arts, Qi Gong travelled to the United States, Britain, Germany and France.

On this trip he saw many great works of art, including the justly famous Chinese painting in the British Museum known as *The Admonitions of the Palace Instructress*, attributed to Gu Kaizhi (*c.*345–*c.*406). However, it was the transatlantic flight on Concorde that became his favourite recollection. This was, perhaps, not altogether unexpected, since there has always been a very 'modern' streak in this proudly conservative calligrapher. He was among the first in China to become an enthusiastic user of the mobile phone, and he has long been a keen collector of cuddly toys – one of his favourites being a stuffed 'Ninja Turtle', which delights both him and his visitors (see fig. 93).

Qi Gong remains one of the delightful anomalies of modern China. He is the only surviving close relative in China of the last emperor, his scholarship is widely admired, and he has brought cheer to literally hundreds of thousands of people with his colourful humour. Through his skill with a brush and his facility with words, this untypical aristocrat has done so much not just to revive the art of calligraphy, but also to give it a greater popular appeal than it has ever had before.

WANG SHIXIANG

1914–

The reluctant calligrapher

95 In his research Wang is ably supported by his wife Yuan Quanyou, a distinguished musicologist. The painting in the background of this photograph shows Wang when he was working on a farm during the Cultural Revolution.

Wang Shixiang is one of China's most stylish calligraphers and greatest scholars of the arts. His calligraphy is marked by an elegance that harks back to previous ages, while his poetry reflects an exuberance for life and is full of acute observations. What is more, he is blessed with a mild temperament that has enabled him to keep smiling in the face of repeated adversity. Despite the admiration that others express for his work, Wang adamantly denies that he is a calligrapher. Nevertheless, he always keeps brushes on his desk and uses them frequently.

A man of many arts

Wang grew up in Beijing, where he spent a happy, even pampered childhood. His parents were cultured, prosperous and liberal-minded. His father was a well-to-do senior diplomat and his mother had the rare distinction of being one of the few young women from Imperial China to study painting in Paris and London.

Wang's parents let him keep falcons, pigeons, fighting crickets and dogs. From an early age he was fascinated by how objects were made and things were done. He loved talking to those who knew the answers, regardless of their social standing. For example, it was from the Mongol wrestlers who had belonged to the Court before the revolution of 1911 that he learned the secrets of badger hunting!

153

Wang's education was quite cosmopolitan. He attended first the American School in Beijing and then Yanjing University (later to become Beijing University). At these establishments he acquired a remarkable command of English, which is still slightly tinged with Americanisms, as well as an enthusiasm for both basketball and soccer.

At university Wang quickly gained a reputation for being somewhat eccentric. He became known as the student who took chirping crickets into class, who appeared one day with an eagle on his arm, and who often wore peasant clothes at a time when his fellow students were snazzily attired in Western dress. Despite this light-hearted approach to life, however, he proved himself a serious student of Chinese literature. It soon became clear that he possessed other skills, too, including an ability to write enchanting poetry and elegant calligraphy.

The pleasures of life in Beijing diminished sharply in 1937 when the Japanese occupied the city at the beginning of the Sino-Japanese War. Nevertheless, Wang was able to continue his postgraduate work on the aesthetic theory of Chinese painting. In 1943, his research finished, he made the difficult journey to the village of Lizhuang, 500 kilometres up the Yangzi River from China's wartime capital, Chongqing, to join the Society for Research in Chinese Architecture, which had been transferred there on the outbreak of war.

Following the defeat of Japan in 1945, Wang was commissioned by the Chinese Government to retrieve the many national treasures that had been looted during the occupation, by the Japanese and others. He fulfilled the task so well that he was rewarded with a position in the Palace Museum, and in 1948 he won a one-year Rockefeller Scholarship to the United States and Canada. He returned to China just as the Communists were gaining control of the country. In 1951 he was imprisoned on the grounds that he must somehow have profited from his work in recovering looted objects – a charge Wang vehemently denied. Ten months later, having failed to find any evidence against him, the authorities reluctantly released him, He was not allowed to return to the Palace Museum, but the Institute of Music readily gave him a post.

Politics soon caught up with Wang again. In 1957 he was condemned as a 'Rightist' for having criticized earlier political campaigns and for complaining about the way he had been treated, as well as about the lack of trained staff to look after cultural relics. His punishment was fairly light, however. He was criticized publicly, but allowed to keep his job. Five years later, in 1962, he was relieved of the epithet 'Rightist' and sent to the Research Institute of Art Objects and Museums.

In the 1950s Wang began work on a series of projects that were to bring him renown years later. As his friend Hu Shiping put it, he started 'combing the beaches of Chinese culture for the gems either unknown, overlooked, neglected or even looked down upon by others'. Above all, Wang concentrated on exploring the practical aspects of various arts which had hitherto fallen outside the interest of most scholars. However, as time went by he realized that, as a result of modernization and social change, China was in danger of losing the last of its great craftsmen who were the traditional practitioners of such arts. He therefore determined to tap and document this valuable source of knowledge before it was too late.

Wang's approach to this task stemmed from his youthful enthusiasm for discovering how things worked or were done. The hallmark of his scholarship has always been the combination of detailed historical research with a deep understanding of the technical issues involved in creating a work of art. His first book was on Chinese lacquerware, which he researched by talking directly to the craftsmen who made it. They responded eagerly to his admiration of their skills and to his unpretentious manner.

Outside of his work, one of Wang's main interests was collecting Ming furniture – a passion that could be easily satisfied in the early years of New China as fine pieces which had once belonged to the well-to-do began to appear in proletarian second-hand shops. Since their return to Beijing from Lizhuang in 1945, Wang and his wife had been living in a fine Ming dynasty courtyarded house just within the eastern city wall. Although in the mid-1950s the authorities insisted that they rent out part of the house, there was still enough space to accommodate their collection, which continued to expand with the increasing availability of fine pieces.

The Cultural Revolution

As the violence of the Cultural Revolution steadily grew in 1966 and 1967, the Wangs realized that they were soon likely to become its victims. As a safeguard, they decided to make their priceless furniture collection less vulnerable to the destructive forays of the Red Guards. Because Wang knew so much about how Ming furniture was constructed, he was able to take each item apart, pack the individual pieces of wood flat and lash them tightly together with rope. In this way, the fragile furniture was rendered virtually unbreakable.

In the event, the Red Guards who eventually came to harass the couple were from the research institute at which the Wangs both worked. These youths were therefore less intent on destroying things than other Red Guards would have been. Instead, they preferred to seize property 'in the

155

name of the people', which in essence amounted to storing valuable objects in a kind of 'cultural depot'. Once Wang's furniture had been carted away, the space that had been vacated was soon occupied by Red Guards who chose to lodge in the house, leaving him and his wife little more than a closet in which to live.

Worse was yet to come. Like millions of other officials and intellectuals, the Wangs were soon sent to the rural 'cadre schools' connected with the organization that employed them. The purpose of this move was to force them to 'improve themselves' by working with the peasants. The Cultural Bureau that supervised the Research Institute of Art Objects and Museums had two such 'schools' – one south of Wuhan in central China and the other not far from Tianjin, the port serving Beijing. Wang was sent to the former, his wife to the latter.

When Wang arrived at the cadre school, he found the conditions harsh. Because he had contracted tuberculosis upon arrival, he was kept isolated from other people and had to live in a shack that had formerly been occupied by pigs. Many of those in the cadre schools became overwhelmed by unhappiness. Wang, however, not only resolved to make the best of things but vowed that, when he finally got out, he would accomplish something worthwhile for every single remaining day of his life. It was in this defiant mood that he composed a short poem about a nearby plot of rapeseed:

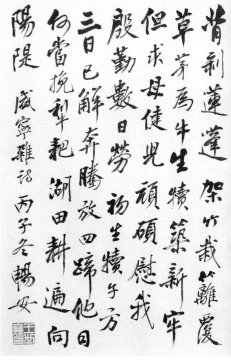

96 Two of the poems Wang wrote during the Cultural Revolution about the pair of water buffalo he was responsible for tending, with which he established a good relationship.

> *Though the storm ravaged the rapeseed,*
> *breaking its stalk and pulling up its roots;*
> *it lifted its head proudly and continued to bloom.*
> *Surely, it swore, I shall bear rapeseed in abundance.*

A little later, Wang sought to ease the pain of being cut off from his beloved research by closely observing the pair of water buffalo he had been tasked with looking after. They soon became one of the great pleasures of his rural existence and inspired him to write four short poems, which, even though they used classical language, were easy for most people to understand (fig. 96). One of them read as follows:

> *I've watched them carefully, I know their tastes...*
> *When I take them out, they know they will get just what they want.*
> *As the sun goes down we plod leisurely homewards along the dyke,*
> *enjoying the evening breeze.*
> *I know that I'm really too old to be riding facing backwards*
> *and eating lotus seeds like a country boy,*
> *But kindly don't spoil my pleasure by laughing at me.*

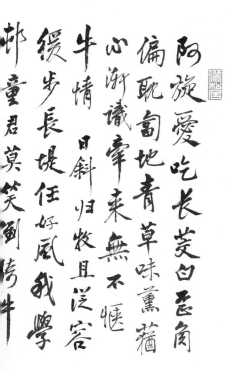

Having been a gourmet in his youth, Wang learned to be an excellent cook in middle age, making the most of the little food available. In order to obtain the best ingredients he would be among the first in line early in the morning outside the state-owned food stores, where most of his companions in the queue were the cooks who had worked in Beijing's finest restaurants. He chatted to them about cooking and recipes so often, and so knowledgeably, that many of them thought he, too, was a professional cook.

Wang's culinary skills stood him in good stead at the cadre school, as did the knowledge of wild herbs, fruits and vegetables that he had acquired in his youth. He would regularly surprise his fellow 'inmates' by preparing gastronomic treats. On one of his forages for ingredients he even found a rare herb that enabled him to prepare a dish that was said not to have been made since the days of the Qian Long emperor.

Wang had mixed emotions about being detained in the countryside. The longer he stayed there, the closer he felt to the ongoing wonders of nature. Nevertheless, he was angered by the thought of losing so much time that he could have spent on research. When, in 1973, he learned that he would soon be allowed to return home, he expressed his feelings at the prospect in the following poem (see also fig. 16 on p. 26):

> *In the spring, I collect wild orchids,*
>> *and in the autumn, the cloud-like mushrooms*
>>> *that are the 'food of fairies'.*
>
> *For lunch, I eat little soft-shelled turtles*
>> *and for supper, the best freshwater fish.*
>
> *Day after day, I wander happily,*
>> *without work or cares.*
>
> *But I resent the fact that I have been*
>> *wasting so much precious time.*

For anyone familiar with the highlights of classical Chinese poetry, this piece strikes a powerful chord. Wang's final words are the refrain from the *Requiem* by the much-loved poet Qu Yuan (340–278 BC), who had been banished by the king whom he had been advising. The refrain of the requiem is all about his urgent need to return to his post.

A renewed enthusiasm for life

Back in Beijing, life for Wang and his wife (who had returned from the countryside at roughly the same time) gradually became more normal, especially after the overthrow of Jiang Qing and her supporters in 1976.

The Wangs spent much of their time renewing their links with old friends, some of whom had fared less badly than they had, while others had suffered far more.

Before long, Wang and his wife regained full possession of their former accommodation. To their great surprise, their huge and priceless collection of furniture was also returned to them intact. By a stroke of good fortune, Wang's tightly lashed stacks of wood had been taken to the Temple of Confucius (an appropriate resting place for the possessions of such a distinguished scholar) before it was bricked up to protect it from the Red Guards. There the furniture had remained for several years, neglected but safe.

With prodigious energy, Wang settled down to write two major books on Ming and early Qing furniture, *Classic Chinese Furniture* (1985) and *The Connoisseurship of Chinese Furniture* (1989). Both volumes were translated into English and other languages and met with international acclaim. Soon Wang began to receive visits from many foreign scholars of Chinese furniture, who were amazed to see that such an extraordinary collection had survived the Cultural Revolution. During this period Wang had some of his best pieces elegantly displayed in his study, where he would pose for photographs dressed in a traditional long Chinese gown.

As time went by and the range of his research widened, piles of books and papers began to obscure the view of his furniture collection. Nevertheless, in winter he always reserved a special place by the stove for his singing crickets (which lived in the gourd cricket boxes that Wang himself had made for them), and he never failed to find room on his desk for the orchids and other flowers that he tended throughout the year.

In 1982 Wang was invited to Britain by the Victoria & Albert Museum and there he met Craig Clunas, a young curator of Chinese art. They both lamented the dismal state of research on so many of the minor Chinese arts. Over the next few years Wang set about addressing the issue by publishing books on pigeon whistles (1989), decorative gourds (1993), bamboo carving (1997), crickets (1999) and pigeons (2000), as well as dozens of articles on an even wider range of subjects. A few of these articles were about cookery, and some of Wang's friends hoped that he would write more about food, especially as he had been one of the judges of China's first National Cooking Contest in 1983. But as long as they were able to continue to enjoy the dishes he prepared, they did not press the point.

The authorities had come to hold Wang in such high regard that he was among the group of scholars and artists that Deng Xiaoping appointed to the Chinese People's Political Consultative Conference (CPPCC), a largely honorific body, membership of which conferred a certain social status upon

97 In this poem Wang expresses his pleasant surprise at the warm welcome he received on his first visit to Xinjiang province in the far west of China.

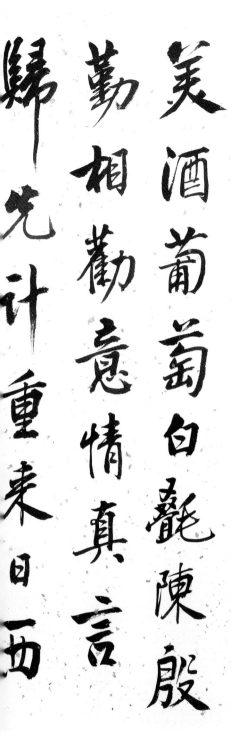

那些 invited to join its ranks. Wang was initially appointed in 1983, then reappointed for a further four-year term in 1987 and again in 1991.

Among the benefits of membership of the CPPCC were the official visits to different parts of the country. In the late 1980s Wang joined the group that went to the grape festival at Tulupan (Turpan), in Xinjiang province. On the way there they drove through the so-called 'Sunset Pass', which the Chinese traditionally regard as the western limit of their civilization, beyond which lie the harsh lands of Central Asia.

When the Tang poet Wang Wei (701–761) described this pass in his poem *Departure*, he lamented that once his friend had crossed it he would never meet anyone he knew. Wang, conversely, so enjoyed himself at the grape festival at Tulupan that he decided to write a poem called *Returning* (fig. 97), composed of lines from Tang poetry but with the negative mood changed to a positive one. It dealt with the pleasurable prospect of one day returning west of the Sunset Pass:

> *On the white coverlet there are fine grapes and wine.*
> *We drink to seeing each other another time.*
>
> *We are already thinking of returning here,*
> *where we now have old friends and such good cheer.*

In 1993, just before Wang's eightieth birthday, the Chinese and English editions of his book *The Charms of the Gourd* were published in Hong Kong. Their preliminary matter included contributions from three of his close friends: a painting of gourds by the artist Huang Yongyu, a poem by Huang Miaozi, and an introduction by Qi Gong describing his impressions of the book.

Qi Gong (pp. 146–52) paid Wang a great Chinese tribute by calling him a 'master of the art of indulging in trivial things without sapping the will'. Through his command of detail, he said, Wang had gained an extraordinary depth and breadth of knowledge. This praise was particularly apt, because Wang had just begun the task of editing a collection of a hundred articles on different aspects of Chinese art and culture that he had written during the preceding fifty years, many of which had never before been formally published.

For years Wang had been thinking about how his collection of furniture could best be preserved for posterity. Since there was no museum in Beijing that would guarantee to display it effectively, he arranged for the collection to go to the Shanghai Museum, which was willing to allocate an entire gallery within the new building it was opening in 1996. The mechanics of this process, however, were somewhat Byzantine: Wang first sold the collection to a Hong Kong tycoon for a fraction of its market value and then the tycoon donated the collection to the museum.

With the money they made from the sale, Wang and his wife were able to move from their old house (which was about to be demolished as part of the redevelopment of Beijing) to a sunny modern apartment in the diplomatic quarter that adjoins the Temple of the Sun. Wang says he has no regrets about not having made more money from his collection, as it would only have made other people envious or provoked them to pester him.

The impending departure of the collection for Shanghai prompted Wang's young friend Sa Benjie to do a painting of one of Wang's famous tables, accompanied by an enchanting story entitled *A Fable about a Table*, which relates the history of this fine piece (see fig. 129 on p. 219).

Although Wang travelled to Hong Kong and Taiwan several times in the early 1990s, he never ventured further afield, despite several invitations to do so. Finally, in 1997, he and Fu Xinian, another great scholar of the Chinese arts, accompanied their mutual friend Qi Gong on a visit to New York, London and Paris. They crossed the Atlantic by Concorde, thus becoming the first distinguished Chinese calligraphers to travel faster than the speed of sound. In London they visited the British Museum, where they were shown the famous scroll known as *The Admonitions of the Palace Instructress*, perhaps the most famous early Chinese painting to have survived. On his return to Beijing, Wang settled down to finish the editing of his hundred articles for publication.

The art of a non-calligrapher

To celebrate Wang's eightieth birthday in 1994, his wife made a large and beautifully composed papercut illustrating fifteen of the arts and interests that had delighted her husband over the years. Among them were furniture, lacquerware and music. Curiously, however, the art of calligraphy was omitted.

Wang himself claims that calligraphy is not one of his passions, nor a subject to which he feels he has made any original contribution. One of his favourite seals reads: 'I much regret that I did not learn calligraphy earlier.' Even so, he concedes that in the 1930s his calligraphy was 'very charming' and 'quite handsome'. Qi Gong, in his introduction to *The Charms of the Gourd*, describes Wang's calligraphy as being 'in the perfect style of Ouyang Xun', the renowned sixth-century calligrapher.

Wang claims that he is only ever invited to do calligraphy either because of the indulgences of friendship or because he is a well-known scholar.

The Chinese tradition, he points out, is to 'respect the calligraphy because you respect the person' (*shu yi ren zhu*). His friends contest this view. They say that the pleasure they receive from Wang's calligraphy stems from the fact that, while he knows the rules well, he now feels sufficiently free to break some of them. Moreover, he is unwilling to fuss too much over his calligraphy. The result is that he spaces his characters well on the paper, but they each have a slightly rough edge to them, which gives them visual interest and excitement. As Sa Benjie puts it, Wang's calligraphy provides 'the pleasure of watching a soccer champion rather than a ballerina'.

Wang's calligraphy is much admired, even outside the wide circle of his friends. In 1997, for example, the organizers of a special exhibition in Taiwan of modern Chinese calligraphy on Buddhist themes chose to use Wang's piece to decorate both the front and back covers of their catalogue. The following year the Museum of Chinese History, having belatedly decided to start collecting the works of contemporary calligraphers, asked Wang to contribute a piece. He responded by writing out the poem he had composed towards the end of the Cultural Revolution in which he laments the years of his life that were wasted (see p. 157).

(see p. 157)

In 1999 it became more difficult still for Wang to deny his calligraphic talent when a book was published containing almost a hundred of his poems, written out mainly in his own hand. Some of them demonstrate his enduring ability to create delightful variations on the style of Ouyang Xun. Others are done in a running script, with strong tapering vertical strokes reflecting the inspiration of Wang Xizhi, the most admired of all Chinese calligraphers.

More than a quarter of a century ago Wang promised himself that if he ever got out of the cadre school he would achieve something worthwhile every day. He has more than lived up to this bold pledge. He has demonstrated a rare talent for understanding the practical aspects of creating works of art, and shown a deep insight into the culture of which they are a part. This is also true of his calligraphy, which – like his poetry – injects into the classical tradition an uncommon zest for life.

6 THE MODERNISTS

WANG DONGLING
1945–

The painterly calligrapher

98 Wang Dongling is renowned for his large-scale works.

By combining classical Chinese styles with inspiration from other arts and cultures, Wang Dongling has shown how calligraphy can become a wonderfully creative, modern art. He admires Picasso, Klee, Miró and Matisse for their ability to express their feelings through linear means. As line is the essence of Chinese calligraphy, Wang believes that experimenting with it can not only refresh Chinese art, but also contribute to the development of a new international genre.

Learning calligraphy during the Cultural Revolution

Wang originally intended to be a painter. He entered the department of fine arts at the teachers' college in Nanjing, the capital of his home province of Jiangsu, when he was just seventeen years old. Rather unusually for the time, the course in which he was enrolled devoted a considerable amount of time to calligraphy. In retrospect, Wang feels that this was his first step on the road to becoming a calligrapher.

The college was closed soon after the Cultural Revolution began in the summer of 1966. Wang was first sent to work in a printing works and then transferred to the local cultural and educational office, which had been charged with promoting mass education through art. Wherever he went, Wang took his brushes and paper with him.

This habit soon landed him in trouble, as the content of his calligraphy was still based on classical Chinese poems. Not surprisingly, he was criticized for being 'feudal, capitalist and revisionist in outlook'. But because he was young, quick to acknowledge his 'mistakes' and accomplished at writing big-character posters, he escaped punishment. Wang believes that his experience of writing posters amid the fervour of the Cultural Revolution released him from the tight discipline imposed in the calligraphy classes at college. For the first time, he felt a real sense of artistic freedom.

Ironically, the wanton destruction of all forms of traditional art that took place during the Cultural Revolution provided a means by which Wang's eyes were opened yet more to the beauty of calligraphy. The ransacking of private collections by the Red Guards resulted in a large number of works of calligraphy and calligraphic copybooks appearing in the streets, destined for destruction by the mob. Canny students of the art were often able to salvage fine pieces or buy them at ridiculously low prices from those who had picked them up. Wang cherishes to this day the calligraphy he acquired during those years.

His passion for calligraphy was further increased when, in late 1968, he slipped away from his propaganda work to Wujiang, where he joined a group of students who were being taught by Lin Sanzhi (pp.140–5), one of modern China's greatest calligraphers. As far as the locals were concerned, this group was learning how to promote 'proletarian culture' more effectively through calligraphy. In practice, they were learning the secrets of this ancient art.

Exposure to new ideas

At the end of the Cultural Revolution in 1976, Wang returned briefly to his college to collect his degree. By then he was determined to pursue a career as a calligrapher. He decided to attend the Zhejiang Academy of Art (now the National Academy of Art) because of illustrations he had seen of the work of Lu Weizhao (1899–1980), who was the professor of calligraphy there. As Wang himself once told me, he felt that Lu's calligraphy 'gripped you because it had a unique combination of brushwork and structure that was uplifting to all who saw it'.

When he enrolled at the Academy in 1979, Wang was disappointed to find that his main teacher was not Lu but the calligrapher-scholar Sha Menghai (pp. 133–8), who was head of the provincial museum and had recently been appointed a professor at the Academy. But this initial disappointment soon faded as he came to admire Sha's ability to convey an inner strength by the use of bold and energetic brushstrokes.

Through his close contact with Sha, Lu and Lin Sanzhi, which lasted for several years, Wang was exposed to three noticeably different perspectives on the art of calligraphy. Sha was a master of the classical technique, who paid attention to the construction of individual characters. Lu, who never liked following the rules of others, had already broken free from the mould of traditional calligraphy and was combining clerical and seal script into a new form that was full of movement. From his contact with Lin, Wang gradually saw how studying and copying the works of earlier masters could refresh one's own creative powers. He likened it to the way in which mastery of classical art had provided Picasso and Matisse with a firm understanding of the structure of the human form, upon which they were able to base their later abstract work.

Besides accepting Lin's view that a knowledge of classical calligraphy gives you the freedom to find your own path, Wang also came to share his

Detail of fig. 101

belief that the essence of the art is the projection of the personality of the artist. In Lin's case, this 'personality' reflected a rare mix of the meticulousness of the scholar and the spontaneity of a child. But above all, he had an inner strength of character that imbued his calligraphy with a deeply spiritual dimension and lent force to the rhythmical movement of his lines. Wang was quick to grasp Lin's point that if he were to succeed in creating a distinctive, free-ranging cursive script, then he would have to base his work on his own intuition and individual spirit.

During his early years at the Academy, Wang was strongly influenced by the works of one of the great masters of the past, Xu Wei (1521–93), who had expressed his feelings in an excitingly fresh style that often combined the flamboyant with the naïve. As China began to open up in the early 1980s, Western art became better known. Books were published on many leading Western artists, and in addition Wang was able to learn a great deal about modern art from the foreign students to whom he taught calligraphy at the Academy.

As the 1980s progressed, Wang began to feel that he had a mission to try to revitalize the art of calligraphy. He knew of recent developments in the work of the Modernist school, who held a major exhibition in Beijing in 1985, but what they were doing was not to his taste. He therefore started to explore different avenues. As he explains in his book *The Art of Calligraphy* (1986), he believed above all that the revival of calligraphy depended on its becoming more painterly. Traditionally, critiques of calligraphy had tended to focus more on the personality of the artist than on his technique. Greater emphasis, Wang argued, now needed to be given to the issues of technique and composition.

He also felt that Chinese calligraphy had become too inward-looking. Even though it was deeply rooted in Chinese culture, few people recognized it as a fine art. Wang proposed not only that calligraphy should be regarded as a fine art in its own right, but that as such it should be treated as an integral part of the whole spectrum of the arts, throughout both China and the West. The time had come, albeit belatedly, for China to embark on the process of revitalizing calligraphy. There was no need to fear the influence of foreign art, as it could easily be absorbed within an art form that would always retain its Chinese essence.

The years 1987 and 1988 were highly creative ones for Wang. There were two major exhibitions of his work, first in Hangzhou and then in Beijing. Several of the exhibits demonstrated his traditional calligraphic skills. Others were more 'Modernist' in form – for example, his calligraphy done on newspaper or as part of a collage. During this period he also

165

produced his first two large-scale works. The first and best known is *Ru, Dao, Fo* ('Confucianism, Daoism and Buddhism'), which represents the three main roots of Chinese culture. Although this piece measures 265 × 205 cm, it was soon completely dwarfed by a work that one might call his 'View from Heaven': ten huge characters in bold cursive script on four panels which, in total, measured 360 × 720 cm.

In this massive work Wang wanted to show that by placing words on paper in a painterly way one could greatly enhance their impact (see fig. 50 on p. 56). His choice of subject underscores this intent. The characters are taken from a poem by Ruan Ji (210–263), who evokes the grandeur of China's landscape by imagining what one might see looking down from Heaven:

> *The towering Mount Tai looks as small as a grindstone,*
> *While the mighty Yellow River snakes its way across the land*
>   *like a silken cord.*

Wang would have liked to paint this piece to the sound of Chinese music, but he felt it demanded something more stirring. He finally decided on Dvořák's *New World Symphony*, playing it at full volume on his recently acquired 'ghetto-blaster' as he took up his huge brush and plunged into the creation of his composition. Wang was amused by the thought that music composed by a European about the American landscape was inspiring a Chinese artist (who at that point had never travelled outside his own country) to create the largest piece of calligraphy ever executed in China.

Foreign experiences

During the late 1980s and early 1990s Wang's art was to be greatly influenced by the very different cultural environments he experienced in the United States and Japan. The former led to his style becoming more open and international; the latter served to remind him that his art would only succeed if it remained firmly rooted in Chinese culture and the traditions of Chinese brushwork.

When Wang was appointed a visiting professor of calligraphy at the University of Minnesota from 1989 to 1992, it was the first time he had ever visited a Western country. It proved to be a traumatic experience. Not only was everything new to him, but he spoke no English and his colleagues seemed always to be too busy to help him learn. He began to understand what true loneliness was. At the same time, however, his art received a considerable boost from his new surroundings. In the great art museums of America there was every opportunity to study Western paintings and

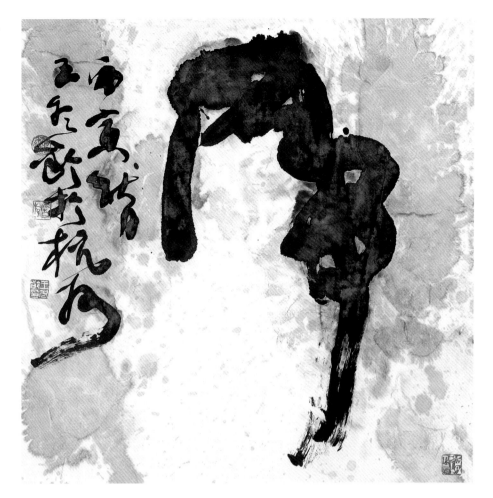

99 In *Tiger* (1986) Wang broke with convention not only by writing that character in a particularly powerful form of cursive script, but also by setting it against a specially coloured background.

discover the power they conveyed through composition, line and colour. Moreover, in the vast expanses of North America he came into closer contact with the wonders of nature than he had in China.

Wang encountered numerous difficulties in trying to teach calligraphy to students who knew neither the Chinese language nor how to use a Chinese brush. Ironically, these problems catalysed further changes in his approach to his own work. By emphasizing the links between abstract art and Chinese calligraphy, he was able to develop new forms of composition that were closer to painting – both Chinese and Western – than to traditional calligraphy (fig. 99). Within the calligraphy he did at this time there are no characters, readable or otherwise, but he always adds a title to guide the viewer's thinking about his brushwork.

Whilst in the United States Wang mounted several solo exhibitions of his work. He also produced the title banner for the 'Sacred Mountains' exhibition of Chinese art held at New York's Metropolitan Museum of Art in 1993. Among his new pieces were several innovative collages that integrated Western images with Chinese characters to form a composition expressing a simple concept. For example, over a collage containing a photograph of the legendary Martha Graham dancing, he wrote the character for 'dance' in bold black strokes. In smaller, finer characters he added

167

a line from a classical poem that describes how seeing a beautiful woman's sword dance greatly improved the cursive script of the Tang artist Zhang Xu (active 710–750).

From time to time Wang continues to make collages. For his *Feeling and Passion* of 1999 (fig. 100) he took two identical spreads from a German arts magazine, turned them sideways, and splashed boldly across each the character *gan* ('feeling'). He then placed the two sheets side by side, but with the left-hand one turned upside down. His intention was to illustrate how 'feeling' becomes 'passion' when, for example, one is 'head-over-heels' in love.

On his return to China in 1992 Wang went to Beijing to work with the Chinese Calligraphers' Association. There he devoted much of his time to studying the ancient masters in order to enhance his technique, which he felt had deteriorated during his time abroad. His longer-term aim, however, was to focus on the purely artistic aspects of calligraphy. Gradually his work won wider acclaim within the Association. Other leading calligraphers began to recognize the depth of his classical training and the extent to which his experiments were, in some respects, a bold continuation of those that had taken place in earlier periods.

100 Wang's dramatic representation of the inverse relationship between 'feeling' and 'passion'.

168

Whilst on a sabbatical in Japan in 1993, Wang was able to study the Chinese calligraphic treasures in Japanese collections, some of which are originals and others copies more authoritative than those in China. One of them was the *Long Chang Si Bei* (the commemorative stone tablet of the Long Chang monastery). Wang spent two hours a day copying the regular script of this sixth-century text by an unknown artist. He was convinced that this exercise was a prerequisite for mastering traditional calligraphy, first running script and then cursive script. It is cursive script for which Wang is now justly renowned.

Creating a language of his own

After his sabbatical in Japan, Wang returned to the Academy in Hangzhou, where he was appointed professor of calligraphy. The following year he staged an exhibition with the title 'Exploring Modern Calligraphy' at the China Art Gallery in Beijing, which consisted mainly of his own works but also included exhibits by a number of his students. Wang's own pieces on display, which spanned the years 1987 to 1993, demonstrated not only his skill as an artist but also his extensive knowledge of Chinese history and philosophy, especially Daoism and Zen Buddhism. Many of them were subsequently illustrated in *The Art Works of Wang Dongling*, a high-quality art book that Wang himself published in 1994 at a personal cost of 170,000 yuan (US$20,000), a huge sum in China at that time.

Wang remains committed to pursuing the task set by his mentor, Lin Sanzhi – to work outside of the limits of tradition in order to find ways of expressing one's own feelings. In doing this, he hopes to broaden the parameters of traditional Chinese calligraphy. One of the basic aspects of the art that Wang has developed most productively is his control of brush and ink. Obviously, what he writes exists in two dimensions, but by varying the density of the ink and the speed of his brushstrokes, he is able to create characters that give an impression of depth – indeed, they seem almost sculptural in form, with the strokes weaving in and out of one another. The textures of his ink are full of fascinating effects that go far beyond what has previously been achieved in Chinese painting, let alone calligraphy. Few can rival the range of tones and effects he manages to achieve. His work, however, is never simply a virtuoso performance of ink and brush; it is always deeply rooted in Chinese culture.

Owing to their scale, Wang's larger pieces cannot be done on a table in the traditional manner. Most often, he works on paper placed directly on the floor, achieving his huge characters by standing on the paper and using a brush as big as a kitchen mop. His less large characters are produced by kneeling on the paper and stretching across it to create the strokes. To maintain the flow of smaller characters, he has to move up and down the paper in a crouching position, which requires him to use his brush at an unorthodox angle.

In the late 1990s, after almost a decade of doing only smaller works, Wang again began to produce very large pieces of calligraphy. He found that working on huge expanses of white paper enhanced his desire to convey his feelings through line and ink. This process is consummated by an outpouring of great energy. It is somewhat like an improvised performance, which by definition can have no rehearsal, as that would detract from the vigour and immediacy of the piece. Success in working on such a scale requires both the courageous spirit of *gongfu* and the self-control that is essential to this martial art. Wang has both of these attributes. Like his mentor Lin Sanzhi, he has trained in the toughest form of *gongfu*, the form followed by the 'fighting monks' of the Shaolin monastery.

One of the strands of ancient Chinese philosophy that has increasingly interested Wang over recent years is Daoism, which holds a deep attraction for many people in modern-day China. It is based on the teachings of someone called Laozi (literally 'the old teacher'), who is believed to have written or compiled the book known in Chinese as the *Daodejing* (hence the name Daoism) and in English as *The Way and its Power*. 'The Way' is described as the source of all existence, the governor of life, and the means whereby all life's contradictions are resolved. The good life is one that flows naturally with the spirit of 'the Way'.

'The Way' advocates that rulers should be sages, who refrain from interfering in the lives of their subjects and guide them back towards the age of innocence. But in a world where the ruler is not a sage, people should retire from public life to perfect their personal purity and intelligence, and seek to live in harmony with 'the Way'.

In 2000 Wang created his largest ever work on Daoism (fig. 101), which measures 272×142 cm. The dramatic character at its centre (see enlarged detail, p. 162) is *wu*, representing the concept of 'nothingness' that lies at the heart of this ancient Chinese philosophy. This character is written against a background of the first two chapters of the *Daodejing*. Its opening lines read:

The way that can be spoken of is not the constant way;
The name that can be named is not the constant name.

Nothingness is known as the beginning of Heaven and Earth;
Being is known as the mother of the myriad of creatures.

101 Wang's brushwork is sometimes reminiscent of the 'iron line' of his teacher Lin Sanzhi, as in this dramatic piece on the theme of Daoism.

RIGHT: Detail

170

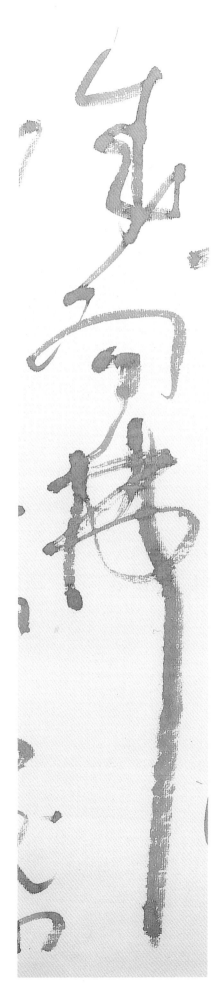

Therefore, always rid yourself of desires
in order to observe the secrets of the way;
But always allow yourself to have desires
in order to observe its manifestations.

In contrast to the central character, which is written with great strength and force, the surrounding text has been rendered in a lively cursive script using a light grey ink – a shade associated more with the palette of the painter than the calligrapher.

Ambitions fulfilled

In the cluttered studio that Wang occupied at the Academy in Hangzhou until it was knocked down for redevelopment in 2000, four photographs faced him from across his desk. One was of a Botticelli painting depicting two shapely women, one was of a youthful Audrey Hepburn, and the other two were of his great hero, Picasso. Ever since he first entered the Academy as a student, Wang has been intrigued by the works of Picasso. In his view the reason why this great Spanish artist so touches the viewer is that he always painted with his soul, and never, throughout his long career, lost his ability to find new forms of expression. When Wang first travelled to Paris in 1998, his main aim was to visit the Picasso Museum. With his long black hair and rather bohemian style of dressing, he looked very much at home on the Left Bank.

Since 1983 Wang's works have been exhibited in Japan, Singapore, Hong Kong, Taiwan, Korea, the United States, Canada, Britain, France, Spain, Germany, Sweden, even Zaire. In Europe his work has made its biggest impact on German artists, who particularly admire his powerful brushwork and his use of black ink, in its many and varied shades, on white paper. In America he is better known than any other Modernist calligrapher still resident in China. Over the past decade he has had ten solo exhibitions in the United States, and his work has featured in three major group exhibitions of Chinese art and calligraphy.

To a greater degree than that of any other leading Chinese calligrapher, Wang's work continues to span the full range of artistic expression, from the Grand Tradition and its Neo-Classical variants, through Modernist styles where characters are presented in new forms or as part of collages of Eastern and Western art, to the innovativeness of the Avant-Garde. Wang has unquestionably made a major contribution to revitalizing Chinese calligraphy and creating an art that can be appreciated by viewers all over the world.

HUANG MIAOZI

1913–

A brush with 'spiritual power'

Among China's modern calligraphers Huang Miaozi is, despite his diminutive stature, a towering figure in terms of moral authority. Since his youth he has been an intriguing mixture of the old and the new. He is passionate about the Chinese classics, satirical cartoons and respect for personal freedoms. His own cheery vitality contrasts sharply with the cruel treatment meted out to him twice in the past five decades.

Satire and nationalism

Huang was raised in a cultured Cantonese family in Hong Kong, where his father struggled to earn a living as the editor of a minor newspaper. At school he had two things drummed into him: the *Analects of Confucius* and that George V was emperor of all the colonies. The arrogance of some of the British he encountered in his youth reinforced the nationalist sentiments he had already acquired from his family, who had once been active supporters of the efforts of China's first President, Sun Zhongshan (Sun Yatsen, 1866–1925) to reform China. By studying Chinese culture, Huang felt that he lightened the burden of being a British 'subject'.

He loved calligraphy from an early age, even though he had to practise it in less than ideal conditions. Because his family was so short of money, as a child Huang was obliged to use water on his brush instead of ink and to do his exercises on a slab of brick rather than a sheet of paper. Nevertheless, by the age of eight his calligraphic skills were already much admired. But Huang was not a conventional child prodigy. Within a few years he was producing impish and irreverent cartoons.

When the Japanese attacked China in 1932, the eighteen-year-old Huang was so outraged that he rushed off to Shanghai to enlist. By the time he arrived there, the Chinese Government had decided not to retaliate for fear that this would only give Japan a pretext for further aggression.

Despite his father's protests, Huang stayed on in Shanghai, working as secretary to the mayor of the Chinese part of the city. What really fascinated him, however, was the 'other' Shanghai, run by the Great Powers and protected by them. He saw this as the greatest city in Asia, cosmopolitan in its politics and its vices. Great wealth and appalling poverty existed side by side, but it offered a degree of stability rare in China at that time.

102 Huang Miaozi uses calligraphy as a powerful vehicle for expressing his views on many issues.

In Shanghai the arts were flourishing and Huang was able to make a name for himself as a part-time cartoonist. It was at the Cartoonists' Club there that he first met Yu Feng, a beautiful and talented young woman who was already secretly helping the Communists. She thought him the most delightfully amusing man she had ever met.

With the Japanese onslaught intensifying, in 1938 China transferred its capital to Chongqing, where Huang later became secretary to the governor of the Central Bank. In this capacity he met Zhou Enlai, who was then head of the Communist liaison mission that was ostensibly seeking to co-operate with the Nationalist Government of President Jiang Jieshi (Chiang Kaishek) in stiffening resistance against the Japanese. Zhou took a liking to Huang for his sense of humour and liberal views, as well as for the skills he displayed as a top ministerial secretary.

The war transformed the dull provincial city of Chongqing into China's liveliest cultural centre. Many of the country's leading artists and writers were there. One of the best known was the scholar and writer Guo Moruo (pp. 80–90), who was to become president of the Chinese Academy of Sciences after the Communist takeover. Guo hosted a party to celebrate the engagement of Huang and Yu Feng in 1943.

Hardship and friendship in New China

With China's civil war spreading southwards, in the late 1940s Huang moved back to Hong Kong. In 1949, shortly after the Communists had secured control of the mainland, he accepted their invitation to return to Beijing. For a while he worked in the new government secretariat that was headed by Zhou Enlai, but before long increasing opposition to the employment of non-Party members in sensitive posts led him to leave government service and take up an editorial post at the People's Fine Arts Publishing House.

During the 'Hundred Flowers Movement' of 1956–7, Huang reiterated a popular Chinese expression that translates roughly as: 'Those who rule do not know much, but those whom they rule know a lot.' However, when the subsequent anti-Rightist campaign began, it was not this remark that put him in the greatest danger. The Party was now alleging that the lively group of artists and writers he had belonged to in Chongqing had contained Nationalist spies who were plotting against the Communists.

Huang was immediately branded a 'Rightist' and despatched to north-eastern China for 'reform through labour' – labour so hard that he nearly died. After an arduous twenty months he was sent back to Beijing, probably as the result of direct personal intervention by Zhou Enlai.

Huang returned to a Beijing where much had changed. Although food was scarce following the chaos of the 'Great Leap Forward' of 1958–9, the political atmosphere was less tense. At the Fine Arts Publishing House he was allowed to write biographies of many artists, both ancient and modern. His wife Yu Feng was also heavily involved in the arts as the director of exhibitions at the newly opened China Art Gallery.

The couple were living in a small part of the run-down courtyarded house that belonged to their friend Wang Shixiang (pp. 153–61). One of their neighbours was Ye Gongchuo (pp. 74–9), the former Nationalist politician and scholar to whom Mao had taken such a liking. Huang and Ye saw each other often and liked to relax by discussing calligraphy and art in their native Cantonese dialect. Another of Huang's key friendships during this period was with Zhang Zhengyu (pp. 119–24), a talented decorative artist whom he had first known in Shanghai in the 1930s, and who in the mid-1960s brought a new vitality to traditional Chinese calligraphy.

The pleasures of the 1960s were brief, however. Within a few years Huang and his wife had fallen victim to the Cultural Revolution. Ironically, it was an erstwhile friend, Jiang Qing, who accused Yu Feng of being a 'Nationalist spy' and Huang of acting as her accomplice. It is likely that Jiang turned against the couple because she feared they knew too much about her libertine days as an actress in Shanghai during the 1930s. In 1968 Huang and his wife were imprisoned.

In a sense, Huang's years of confinement transformed him as a calligrapher. Locked within his cell, he would try to maintain his sanity by composing poems, paintings and calligraphy in his mind. One day a burst of sunlight gave the rainwater on the floor of the cell a magical quality by seeming to turn it into the character for 'valley' (*gu*), written in beautifully balanced clerical script. At that moment Huang swore that one day he would try to recapture the effect in his own calligraphy. Not until 1975, however, were Huang and Yu Feng finally released, after seven years in prison. They quietly returned home. Now sixty-two years of age, Huang decided to retire.

Freedom and expression

Over the next few years, Huang derived comfort and inspiration from copying works by earlier masters of calligraphy. When he first worked in his own style, he sought to achieve tranquillity by writing out poems about nature. He soon began to express his reflections on life and on recent events, using different styles to enhance the power of each message: archaic scripts for calm and reflective moods, powerful cursive script to convey joy or anger.

103 This pair of scrolls stressing the importance of maintaining high standards is explained on p. 180.

Huang's desire to use calligraphy as a means of personal expression was given a powerful boost by the dramatic events of 1976. By the spring of 1977, when the Gang of Four had been imprisoned for several months, condemnation of them was encouraged. It was then that Huang wrote out for his friend Yang Xianyi (pp. 265–73) a couplet he had written a year earlier, which summed up their memories of the thousands of white paper flowers and banners they had seen in Tiananmen Square and the predictions they had made about the fall of the Gang of Four. The sense of it is:

> A hundred thousand wild flowers
>   have been scattered as in a dream.
> Now the will of the people,
>   with the elemental force of wind and thunder,
>   shall determine China's fate.

The tense, almost angry, strokes in this very Classical piece (see fig. 46 on pp. 52–3) reflect the indignation of a man wronged. At the same time, the strength of the characters and the sureness with which they are placed on the paper convey the conviction of a man confident that justice and history are on his side.

Another great impetus to the development of Huang's style was the death of his old friend Zhang Zhengyu. Huang had always been so over-awed by Zhang's great talent that he had been reluctant to stretch his own potential as an experimental Modernist. With Zhang's passing, he felt free to pick up the reins and try to push Modernist calligraphy beyond the point to which Zhang had already taken it.

The new mood of optimism in China revived Huang's naturally sunny temperament. Deng Xiaoping was setting China on a reformist course and making amends for past wrongs. As part of this programme, the authorities provided Huang and his wife with a spacious flat in a new suburb to the east of Beijing, to which they invited many of their old friends. In 1983 Huang was appointed to the Chinese People's Political Consultative Conference (CPPCC) along with other scholars and artists of his acquaintance who had suffered during the Cultural Revolution. Becoming a member of this rubber-stamp body brought him a measure of prestige, as well as certain 'perks', including visits to Japan.

Artistically, Huang was at first excited by Japan. He liked the way the Japanese had already shaped their calligraphy into quite modern forms. To him it seemed almost like abstract art created with Chinese ink, comprising ideas that he was already exploring within his own work. He was also delighted to meet several of Japan's leading modern calligraphers and

175

abstract artists. However, the more he saw of Japanese calligraphy, the more he felt that it lacked both the strength and the depth of content of its Chinese counterpart.

A more important factor in the further development of Huang's art was his participation in the highly controversial exhibition of Modernist calligraphy held in Beijing in 1985. What made Huang's work stand out from many of the other exhibits was the lyricism of his characters and the inter-relationships between them. He brought a vitality to ancient seal-script characters by writing them with speed and fluidity. In addition, he made his works look more like paintings by breaking with the tradition of writing characters in regular columns and instead placing them on the paper in freer artistic arrangements.

One of the main works that Huang contributed to the exhibition was entitled *Great Changes*. Reflecting the optimism of the time, it bore the ancient four-character phrase that means 'Great changes are taking place in the world and in the thoughts of men'. It was very similar to his 1993 version of the same text, which he had set against the background of an elephant (fig. 104). It is often assumed that the elephant has some symbolic significance associated with Chinese history and tradition. Huang, however, insists that his use of the motif was a mere whimsy, prompted by the fact that the character *xiang* ('manifestation' or 'phenomenon') in the composition can mean 'elephant' and its shape vaguely resembles one.

As pleased as Huang was by the changes taking place during this period, experience had taught him that it was all too easy, especially in China, to be taken by surprise. In his view it was only possible to overcome the vicissitudes of life by being true to oneself. He made this point in a pair of scrolls to which he lent added weight by using large characters formed in an archaic style. The text of the piece reads:

Today's time flows by like running water.
But, in my life, I should have the constancy of the bright moon.

The Chinese frequently use the moon as a symbol of constancy, as this is epitomized by the regularity of its phases. In the commentary that Huang wrote on these scrolls he noted that an ancient Greek philosopher once said that 'a man may stand in a river, but the water moves on'. Characteristically, he then added a further comment to underscore the unpredictability of life: 'The radio announced that we would now be having the first snow of winter, but instead the sunshine is as bright as in the spring.'

Huang's first book of calligraphy, published in 1988, contained more than seventy of his works. They show his mastery of the art of calligraphy,

104 Huang's fresh approach to the rendering of ancient characters reinforces the message of this piece, that great changes are taking place in the world and in the thoughts of men.

which has allowed him to create intriguing effects through the use of different densities of ink and varying degrees of dryness of the brush. Equally important has been his ability to combine the exploration of new forms of expression with a depth of knowledge of Chinese poetry and culture that few can match. Not only has Huang demonstrated great skill in selecting apposite quotes from his prodigious knowledge of the classics, but he has written poems of his own in the classical tradition. Although at times deeply moving, more often than not his poetry has a satirical edge.

In the opening pages of Huang's book there is a photograph of him looking amiably resolute as he stands proudly in front of a pair of scrolls.

The scrolls bear the lines:

Sail the boat out through the surging ocean.
Rein in the horse right on the edge of the precipice
    at the top of Mount Kunlun.

To Chinese readers the message is clear. Mount Kunlun is one of China's great sacred peaks, located on the eastern flank of Tibet. In ancient literature it marked the edge of the known world. This couplet therefore reflects the courageous streak in Huang's character, which on several occasions has dramatically affected his life. In retrospect, it seems like an omen.

Speaking out and exile

At the end of the 1980s Huang found himself embroiled in politics. As the crowds swelled in Tiananmen Square in late May 1989, he spoke out strongly in support of the protesters during an interview with a Hong Kong journalist. His remarks carried all the more weight because he was a member of the CPPCC. They were widely quoted in the foreign media.

Following the suppression of the demonstrations on 4 June, Huang and Yu Feng fled to Australia. Life there was not easy for them at first, and even after they settled in more comfortably, Huang still deeply resented the fact that he had been compelled to leave his native country.

Whilst waiting for an opportunity to return home, in 1992 Huang went to Germany. There he met up again with his young friend Gu Gan (pp. 182–92), who, like him, was a visiting fellow at the Heinrich Böll Institute. At the end of that year an exhibition of their works was held at the Museum für Ostasiatische Kunst in Cologne. It was the first major exhibition of modern Chinese calligraphy to be held in either Europe or the United States.

Huang's most memorable piece from this exhibition was inspired by one of Böll's own poems, *Mit diesen Händen* ('With these Hands'), which was the title of the exhibition. It reminded him of the complex times in which he had lived and the questions of conscience still remaining in China. Over the greyish-blue print of an open hand, he wrote part of the poem in the weighty archaic seal script of the Shang-Zhou period (see illustration, p. 10). This is the only example of his work that Huang has refused to sell.

You have washed these hands millions of times
    and they are always clean, pure, innocent.
Nobody has been afraid to clasp them,
    though it was with these hands
    that you placed deadly grenades into the launcher.

105 'The rain-filled clouds cover half the mountain.'

Antipodean inspiration

After Germany, Huang and Yu Feng travelled to Britain, Italy, France, Switzerland, the United States and South Korea. In 1993 they settled in Brisbane, having come to enjoy the quality of life that Australia offered. They liked its subtropical weather and the vibrant colours of the flowers and trees, which at times conjured up for them memories of home. In particular, the heavy clouds that hung on the mountains of Queensland during the rainy season always reminded Huang of China.

In 1992 he set out to capture this mood. First he prepared some paper with a colour-wash that evoked hills and rain, then he wrote across it one of his favourite phrases: 'The rain-filled clouds cover half the mountain.' The characters that Huang used are archaic pictograms (fig. 105), some of which are not hard for a non-Chinese to understand – especially those for rain (bottom right) and mountain (top left).

In Australia Huang had no difficulty in keeping abreast of the latest developments in China, where Deng Xiaoping's reforms were not only creating new opportunities, but also reviving old envies. In the spring of 1994 the antics of one of the magpies in Huang's garden prompted in him a satirical reflection on this situation. The magpie seemed unable to decide which of the many persimmons it wanted to peck at. Huang immediately related this to the large number of Chinese intellectuals who seemed unable to make up their minds whether to remain true scholars or to seek profit from the new economic reforms.

Huang painted a picture showing a hesitant magpie and in front of it several persimmons (fig. 106). These images were perfectly matched, in that the sounds of the Chinese words for magpie (*ya*) and persimmon (*shi*) are the same as those for 'gentlemanly scholar'.

Huang took full advantage of this happy coincidence in the verse he wrote on his painting:

> *The greedy bird gazes at the persimmons*
> > *with the appetite of intellectuals yearning to go into business.*
>
> *Well, if you are really interested in money,*
> > *then go for it like a yuppie, instead of dithering like a scholar.*
>
> *Be a real man!*

106 Poking fun at Chinese intellectuals through the allegory of the magpie and the persimmon.

Return to China

Much as Huang and his wife now enjoyed living in Australia, they still hoped that the improving political climate back home would allow them to return one day. In 1993 they received a message from the Chinese authorities to the effect that they hoped the couple would come back to China. Huang and Yu Feng finally did so the following summer.

In February 1995 the couple staged an exhibition in Beijing covering the full range of their works. The exhibits of Huang's calligraphy included *The Twittering Birds, The Flower in the Rough Ground, With these Hands, Great Changes, The Rain-filled Clouds* and *The Gentlemanly Scholar*, which together presented a clear statement of his views. The opening of the exhibition was a major event, attended by the city's leading artists and art historians. When Qiao Shi, chairman of the National People's Congress and a leading member of the Politburo, subsequently came to see the exhibition, his visit was televised. This was the clearest indication yet that not only was Huang once again fully accepted, but he was highly regarded as an artist.

On this first visit back to China, Huang was unhappy at many of the changes he observed, especially the decline in cultural standards and the rise in corruption. His indignation brought to mind a quotation attributed to Confucius:

> *Through cultivating yourself, you develop a sense of shame.*
> *Through reading widely, you attain broad knowledge.*

Huang wrote out the eight Chinese characters that make up these lines in a style that blends oracle-bone and seal script into one (fig. 103). The combined authority of these two scripts makes the piece appear to convey some divine commandment. Even educated people, however, find the piece difficult to read unless they recognize the quotation.

Over the next few years Huang and Yu Feng divided their time between China and Australia. They remained highly active in both countries, working

107 'Let us…prolong the pleasures of the day into the night.'

180

on their art, organizing exhibitions and writing books. They celebrated the new millennium by buying themselves an apartment in one of the smarter districts of eastern Beijing. Inside, above the front door, is a horizontal plaque bearing two characters written by Huang. When read from right to left in the traditional manner, they bid a polite 'Goodnight' to parting guests. When read from left to right, they mean 'Peaceful old age', which is just what Huang and Yu Feng intend to go on enjoying.

Their definition of peaceful, however, is not what one might expect. They indulge themselves in a schedule of work and play that would tax many people half their age. At the end of 2000 they put on their biggest ever exhibition in China, which included well over a hundred exhibits. It was held in Shanghai, the city where they had first met as smart young people in the Cartoonists' Club in the 1930s.

Huang exhibited several of his latest large pieces. These are based on characters inscribed on the bronze vessels used for ancient rituals, which are brought to life by the bold way in which he renders them and his use of strong, bright colours. For some observers, Huang's strong geometric frameworks call to mind Australian aboriginal art – a form that has long fascinated him. The exhibition was very well received.

Huang and his wife not only continue to work hard, they retain a real zest for life. This perhaps explains why they are so fond of *The Night Feast* by Li Bai (701–762), which Huang feels contains some of the most wonderful images of time and life ever written. Aptly, he decided to write out this poem (fig. 107) for my wife, Kristen Lippincott, the director of the Royal Observatory at Greenwich:

> *The Universe is a lodging house for a myriad things,*
> *and Time itself a travelling guest of the centuries.*

> *As this floating life is like a dream,*
> *let us, like the ancients, light candles and so*
> *prolong the pleasures of the day into the night.*

The interest that Huang's work arouses and the pleasure it gives to so many people is attributable not only to the versatility of his technique, but equally to his wide-ranging knowledge of the Chinese classics, his profound experience of life and politics, and of course his wicked sense of humour. His characteristic determination to make the best of things has, if anything, been heightened by the tragedies and vicissitudes of his own life. As some Chinese critics have observed, the enduring quality of his work is its 'spiritual power' (*ling qi*) – a most appropriate hallmark for a man of Huang's unwavering integrity.

181

GU GAN
1942–

The man who gave meaning to abstract art

Gu Gan gained international recognition in 1998 when he was honoured with an invitation to provide the painting for the label of Château Mouton Rothschild's *grand cru* of 1996. Not only was he the first Chinese artist ever to receive this distinction, but through it he joined an exclusive group of artists including Picasso, Braque, Matisse, Kandinsky, Miró and Hockney, all of whom had produced labels for earlier vintages.

Calligraphy as therapy, then as art

Gu Gan was born into a prosperous family in Hunan province in central China. When he was only three, his father, an officer in the Nationalist Army, was killed while fighting the Japanese. Even so, Gu Gan enjoyed a stable and fairly happy early childhood, growing up in the family home in a hillside village not far from the provincial capital of Changsha.

Following the Communist takeover of China in 1949, Gu Gan's family became desperately short of money. However, with the help of friends in the Communist Party his mother was able to move to Beijing, where she found work as a housekeeper.

Gu Gan's considerable aptitude for painting led to his admission at the age of twenty to China's Central Academy of Fine Arts. But after he had spent two years there, poor health forced him to abandon his studies in Chinese painting. When he recovered, he was assigned to work in the cultural bureau of the Beijing Municipal Government. The advent of the Cultural Revolution led to Gu Gan, along with most of his colleagues, working on the presses in a printing works for the best part of a decade.

The one bright spot in his life was his beautiful girlfriend Zhao Qianqian. However, she became acutely depressed when her father, who had been a Nationalist general, was singled out for harsh treatment by the Red Guards. Ironically, the huge Red Guard rallies in Tiananmen Square provided Gu Gan and Zhao Qianqian with a rare opportunity to meet in relative safety. Here no one paid much attention to two young people whispering to each other. In 1968 the couple married.

Normally, Gu Gan would turn to painting when he wished to relax, but now the stress of daily life was so great that he could not achieve the calm he needed in order to be creative. Instead, he turned to calligraphy. It was

108 In 2000 Gu Gan moved into his new studio, where he has space to work on large pieces of calligraphy.

a move taken not as an alternative route to self-expression, but as a means of achieving a measure of comfort and escape through the repeated and disciplined practice of this art.

In 1975, when life was beginning to return to normal for most people in China, Gu Gan was transferred from the printing works to a position as art editor of the People's Literature Publishing House. In this capacity he was able to resume his study of painting. Within three years he won several prizes for 'outstanding works of art' and was admitted as a member of the Research Academy of Traditional Chinese Painting. During the late 1970s he was allowed to travel extensively in China, from the East China Sea to Tibet, visiting the famous Buddhist sites along the way.

At the same time as he was gaining recognition as a traditional Chinese painter, Gu Gan was becoming increasingly excited by Western art. While at art school he had produced a number of good drawings in the Western style. Before long, his growing interest in modern art led him to focus on Kandinsky, Klee and Miró, whose works were then little known in China. He was fascinated by the extent to which they experimented with the use of line in their efforts to express the beauty of form.

Western art and the revitalization of calligraphy

Through studying Western art Gu Gan came to believe that there were a number of ways in which Chinese calligraphy could be revitalized. From the outset he showed a keen interest in the different effects that could be created from the use of wet or dry brushes and varying densities of ink. By the late 1970s he had begun to adopt a more radical approach to calligraphy, which led to his becoming the prime mover in the Modernist school of Chinese calligraphy.

He started by experimenting with changes in the outer shape of individual characters by elongating or widening them into new forms. His next step was to take characters apart, spreading their constituent elements across his compositions. More radically still, he would write each of these elements in a different script; for example, one in seal script, another in grass script and a third in regular script. Yet another innovation was his use of coloured ink – a dramatic change in an art which traditionally had always been executed in black ink, albeit at times on coloured paper.

Gu Gan and Huang Miaozi (pp. 172–81), his fellow senior editor at an associated publishing house, became increasingly excited at the prospect of reinvigorating calligraphy. In the course of their discussions they came up with the idea of organizing an exhibition of Modernist works. Somewhat to their surprise, the authorities agreed that they could stage one at the China Art Gallery in Beijing. Crowds flocked to see the show when it finally opened in 1985. The works on display broke so many of the conventions of Chinese calligraphy that for supporters and opponents alike the event became a *cause célèbre*.

One of Gu Gan's exhibits was particularly symbolic of the mood of the period and became an icon of the Modernist movement as a whole. In *The Mountains are Breaking Up* (see fig. 48 on p. 55) he drew inspiration from a poem by Li Bai to create a visual metaphor expressing the belief that the time had come for old concepts to be thrown aside and for China to enter a new era. He achieved this through the strength and composition of the two main characters in the piece: in the upper left-hand corner a large character for 'mountain' (*shan*) looked as if it were being overturned by the force of the other main character, *cui* ('destruction' or 'overturning').

This approach marked a major break with tradition. It represented a move towards the idea that the form of a calligraphic composition and the arrangement of the characters within it should reinforce the meaning of the piece. To a greater degree than had previously been seen in Chinese calligraphy, the focus of Gu Gan's work lay in the strength of the overall concept it conveyed, as opposed to poetic imagery or a narrative or allusive stringing together of words.

In recognition of his achievement in mounting the Modernist Calligraphy Exhibition, Gu Gan was elected chairman of the newly established Society of Modern Calligraphy. In this role he devoted a good deal of his time to lecturing about his ideas on modern calligraphy and its links with abstract art. His initial ideas were set out in his book *The Formation of Modern Calligraphy* (1986).

In 1987 Gu Gan travelled to Europe, having been invited to give lectures on modern calligraphy in Bonn, Hamburg and Vienna. While he was at the Hamburg Institute of Fine Arts in Germany, he met Professor K.P. Brehmer, who was fascinated by the changes taking place in calligraphy in China. The two artists have worked together on occasional collaborative pieces ever since.

Greatly encouraged by Professor Brehmer, Gu Gan settled down to write his highly influential book *The Three Steps of Modern Calligraphy*. It was first published in English in 1990 (ably translated by Gu Gan's friend, Professor Hu Yunhuan) with a Chinese-language edition appearing two years later. In the book Gu Gan argues that the ultimate aim of Modernist calligraphy is to provide aesthetic pleasure linked to an idea, rather than following the path of traditional calligraphy, where often lengthy textual content is an essential element of the overall effect.

184

Detail of fig. 22, p. 30
World of Supreme Bliss (1991)

The layers of meaning in Gu Gan's work are created in many different ways. Usually, the title focuses attention on the main subject or theme. It is often also used as an integral part of the composition, be it a single word or a phrase taken from a poem or song. Gu Gan frequently uses pictograms or oracle-bone script to remind the reader of the depth of Chinese history and culture. His decision as to which script to use tends to be linked to the message he intends to convey.

When writing the character for 'autumn' (*qiu*), for example, he might use a warm brown ink in a cursive script, the fragmented form of which reflects what happens to Nature herself as autumn leads on to winter. The impression of decay can be reinforced by the use of 'overnight' ink (see p. 25). This gives a strong central core to each stroke, beyond which the watery ink seeps outwards into the paper, successfully conveying a sense of the fading of autumn into winter. On other occasions Gu Gan writes his characters with so fine a brush that the ink flowing from it almost breaks into dots as the tip of the brush crosses the paper, while the line of the character itself gyrates down and across the paper like a leaf falling after the frost.

Nature and humans are but one

As Gu Gan further explored his own outlook on life in the late 1980s, he was increasingly drawn to the traditional Chinese view that 'nature and humans are but one', sensing that all of nature is constantly trying to resolve itself into a harmonious whole, where opposites are held in balance and extremes reduced. Chinese emperors once used this phrase to support their claim to rule in the name of Heaven. But for Gu Gan and his contemporaries, and many others before them, the phrase relates more closely to the Buddhist idea that all life is precious and there is a need for harmony between mankind and the natural world.

In common with most Chinese, Gu Gan was horrified by what happened in Tiananmen Square in 1989. The following year, as an expression of his wish to see the healing of political wounds, he produced a very subtle composition entitled *The Preciousness of Peace*, which refers not simply to peace between nations but to peace within individual societies. In *Crying Deer*, another of his works of 1990, he highlighted the need for tolerance and mutual understanding. Alluding to the Buddhist belief that the relationship between humans and animals is one of the world's great harmonies, he depicted a mother standing calmly amidst a herd of deer, who cry with delight that she feels at one with them. Both the human figure and those of the deer were modelled on ancient Chinese pictograms.

185

The year 1992 marked one of the milestones in China's long history of reforms. Less than three years after the suppression of the demonstrations in Tiananmen Square, Deng Xiaoping, against the wishes of some of his colleagues, boldly declared that China should again press ahead with economic reform and the expansion of its relations with the West. Deng's call coincided with a fundamental shift in world politics following the collapse of Communism in Central Europe and the Soviet Union.

Gu Gan responded to the events of that year with a work called *A Wish for Universal Peace*, in which he expressed his hopes for future harmony between East and West. This composition is typical of the way in which Gu Gan projects his ideas through the use of only a few characters, with several other symbols reinforcing his basic message. On the left of the piece is a thin-lined version of the Chinese character for 'east' (*dong*), and on the right the one for 'west' (*xi*). Between these two characters are the words 'Open the city gates' (*kai cheng men*). From the top left-hand corner a pictographic eye looks out across the page towards the West, which for the Chinese is another way of referring to America. Elsewhere in the picture Gu Gan uses the character for 'well' (*ding*), a symbol of settled, stable life, together with the Daoist characters for yin and yang, to represent harmony and reciprocity.

Inspiration from Germany

In 1992 Gu Gan and his friend Huang Miaozi were both guests of the Heinrich Böll Institute in Cologne. Gu Gan was greatly stimulated by German art and by his contact with German artists. He liked the abstract work they were doing as well as the strong colours they used.

Between December 1992 and February 1993, works by Gu Gan and Huang Miaozi were on display at the Museum für Ostasiatische Kunst in Cologne. The exhibition's title – *Mit diesen Händen* ('With these Hands') – was not simply a reference to the hands of the two artists, but a homage to the German poet Heinrich Böll, who wrote a poem with the same title in which he explored man's ability to engage in both good and evil acts. Gu Gan and Huang Miaozi each created a work based on Böll's poem. In his, Gu Gan wrote out the words of the poem in Chinese characters against the background of a pair of hands grasping barbed wire, as if desperate to break out of a prison camp into the free world beyond.

Gu Gan's other works exhibited in Cologne demonstrated that whilst in Germany he had taken to using thinner brushstrokes. This created a linear abstract effect recalling the works of Miró, Klee and similar Western painters. Nevertheless, Gu Gan's work remained essentially Chinese. His forms were based on China's oldest script – the thin-lined oracle-bone script that more than 3000 years ago was etched on tortoise shells and the shoulder blades of oxen for the purposes of divination.

Deepening Chinese roots

Gu Gan produced works on Buddhist themes throughout the 1990s. At one level these paintings are quite abstract in that the few characters they contain are difficult to decipher. In most cases, however, the 'text' he uses echoes the title of the piece (which is often a well-known Buddhist phrase), thus rendering the characters easier to understand. The highly innovative use of seals bearing images of Buddha and other Buddhist symbols further strengthens the visual message. Many of these seals, which Gu Gan carves himself, were inspired by his research into the ancient monastery at Dunhuang, whose caves contain lively images that entered China via the Silk Route.

Gu Gan is interested in the concept of the 'heart' in its widest sense. The Chinese word for 'heart' is as rich in meaning as its English counterpart. For Gu Gan, a good rapport between hearts is one of the secrets of harmony and happiness. In his many works on the theme of the heart he has used a wide variety of calligraphic styles and colours to create very different compositions and moods. Sometimes the heart is drawn in thick, dark ink to illustrate strength and commitment. In other instances the strokes of the heart are in a grey 'overnight' ink, with an inner 'bone' and an outer 'flesh' to show that the heart has both strength and softness.

After the political tensions in China had eased, Gu Gan decided to pay tribute to those who over the years, but most notably in 1989, had helped create a better future for others through their own courage. He did so in *Alone in a Vast Wasteland* (1994), which is painted on paper that looks like an aerial photograph of mountains and deserted plains. He has placed a red blotch beside the big, bold character for 'foot', or 'walking', to remind the viewer of the bleeding that accompanies such harsh journeys.

At times Gu Gan has felt dejected because so few people really understand his work. In his 1994 picture *Walking Alone* (fig. 109) he created an abstract composition by using a fine brush to write his message in ancient oracle-bone script, on paper to which he had given a special texture.

I walk the ancient road alone, chilled to the bone,
Then suddenly I have the delight of seeing you.

This was another way of saying: 'I write, but no one seems to understand. How nice it is to meet you, as you are someone who does.'

109 In his 1994 piece *Walking Alone* Gu Gan expresses his gratitude to those who understand his work.

After his return from Germany in 1993, nostalgia featured more prominently in Gu Gan's work. He was now middle-aged and Beijing had become badly polluted. Increasingly he recalled his happy childhood, growing up in a country village. Whilst enjoying the comfort of such nostalgia, at the same time he was actively working with many younger artists in an attempt to enliven the Modernist approach to calligraphy. He devoted tremendous effort to assisting with the organization of the tenth anniversary exhibition of the Modernist movement that was held in Nanjing in October 1995.

For this event Gu Gan produced his work entitled *Opening Up* (fig. 110), which soon came to be regarded as the most important item in the show. His vigorous portrayal of the character for 'opening' (*kai*) left little doubt that the 'door of the old country' mentioned in the inscription had been abruptly opened. Behind the open door, however, is the image of an old house, still in good order, near which perches a *heping* – the bird of peace. This suggests that even with the door open, all has remained well in China. In other words, China has nothing to fear from becoming more closely linked with the rest of the world.

Independence of spirit is a key element in Gu Gan's work. He made this point most forcibly in *My Heart goes out of the Window* (1998). Around the edge of this oil painting he has depicted the dark latticework of a window in a simple Chinese country house, beyond which is bright light. Within that glaring space he has painted the character for 'heart' (*xin*) in different ways. For Gu Gan this work conveys the notion that even if one's body is locked in a particular room, city or country, one's heart and mind can never be so contained. He reinforces this message by starting to draw some of the 'hearts' inside the room and then swirling them out through the window.

Château Mouton Rothschild

It was after seeing his one-man show in London that Baroness Philippine de Rothschild invited Gu Gan to provide a painting to appear on the label of her 1996 *grand cru*. In doing so, she paid homage to a man who had

been pre-eminent in revitalizing the ancient art of calligraphy in modern China. Gu Gan's label was unveiled by the Baroness at a banquet in Hong Kong in the summer of 1998. The black-tie event was attended by hundreds of Companions of the Order of Tastevins dressed in their traditional velvet cloaks, cloche hats and gold chains of office. Gu Gan struggled to appear cheerful from within the confines of his more than usually formal attire. But he knew that the label was a major step forward in his international recognition as an artist.

In designing the wine label, Gu Gan had once again chosen the theme 'heart to heart' (see fig. 54 on p. 61). This time he had intertwined five coloured hearts, each rendered in a different style of calligraphy. The reason for including five hearts was to imply an association with the five inter-linked rings that make up the logo of the International Olympic Federation, which symbolizes cooperation between the five continents.

After a further visit to London in 1999, Gu Gan set off on a pilgrimage to Barcelona to meet the Catalan artist Antoni Tapiès, who had designed the label for Château Mouton Rothschild's 1995 vintage. A prime reason for his wanting to meet this particular artist was that Tapiès had once said: 'We, especially the artists grown up in the school of abstract expression, owe so much to the Chinese calligraphers who enabled us to understand the emotional language of using the skills of the brush.' During their discussions in Spain, Tapiès remarked that in his view the abstract art of each country had its own distinctive flavour. This statement only reinforced Gu Gan's view that the national flavour of Chinese abstract art was strongly rooted in calligraphy.

Gu Gan's visit to London in 1998 sparked off in him an interest in the forthcoming new millennium. He made a special trip to the Old Royal Observatory at Greenwich, where preparations to mark the occasion were already well under way. In advance of the exhibition of his works at Spencer House, London in 1999, he produced a novel piece with the title *Catching Up with Time*. In it, as in some of his other works, he interwove ancient Chinese calligraphy with the traditions of Western modern art.

As a reminder of the transient nature of time, Gu Gan wrote out the year of the millennium celebrations, in Arabic numerals, in a grey ink that he allowed to seep into the paper. Across the number 2000 he superimposed a Chinese pictogram for 'chariot', which dates back over three thousand years. The axle of the chariot runs through the number and is intended to be reminiscent of the Greenwich Meridian, the line from which all time on earth is calculated. Across the bottom of the picture Gu Gan has added wryly: 'A speedy vehicle catching up with time.'

Again marking the advent of the new millennium, Gu Gan did a piece he called *The Age of Red and Gold* in celebration of the success of China's reform movement over the past twenty years (fig. 111). The paper itself represents China, its smoother area denoting the plains and the crumpled effect in the centre the mountains. Although the overall colour is red, its use has no political connotations; red is simply the traditional colour of celebration in China. The black characters make up the ancient form of the Chinese word for 'tree' (*shu*), with the smaller ones accompanied by dots meaning 'fruit' (*guo*), some of which has already ripened into an autumn gold, representing prosperity. The title of the piece is not intended only to summarize China's achievements so far; it also expresses the hope that the country will enter a new Golden Age in the twenty-first century.

Gu Gan greatly enjoys the attention his own work receives internationally, but within China he still feels the need to widen appreciation of the Modernist movement as a whole. To this end, he spent more than a year helping to organize China's largest ever exhibition of Modernist and Avant-Garde calligraphy, the 'Retrospective of Chinese Modern Calligraphy at the End of the Twentieth Century', held in Chengdu in 1999 to mark the end of the old millennium.

Creating a new art form

Over a period of less than twenty years, Gu Gan's art has evolved tremendously. The ideas contained within it have become both deeper and more subtle. He has enhanced the richness of his brush technique by introducing into his works a number of non-traditional materials such as cloth, board and special papers, some of which he makes himself. He now uses acrylic colours, which attain a consistently high level of saturation (whereas Chinese inks tend to soften and recede when the paper is mounted). Since the end of the 1990s he has also experimented with oil paint, although he still has his doubts as to whether it is as good a medium for calligraphy as water-based ink.

Having acquired a spacious new studio in 2000, Gu Gan began working on large pieces of modern calligraphy. Many of them he executed on a recently developed form of *xuan* paper whose unusual thickness and highly textured surface have allowed him to create novel effects. Water from the brush flows quickly on this paper, but its complex structure impedes the distribution of ink particles in an irregular way. Because of the thickness of the paper, the ink also takes a long time to dry. Gu Gan can still be spontaneous in his technique, but the act of creating a large work of art on this new paper has to be performed in at least three separate stages.

Over the years Gu Gan has succeeded in moulding calligraphy and painting into a distinctly new form of art. He has blended together both ancient and modern styles and both Chinese and Western concepts, binding these mixtures with sensitive thoughts about the relationship between man and nature.

Distinguishing him from other leading figures in China's Modernist movement are his interest in abstraction and his ability to turn the conventional relationship between calligraphic form and content inside out. Traditionally, form has served content in Chinese calligraphy, whereas Gu Gan allows the content of a piece to govern its form. A number of other artists have also played on these themes. However, few (if any) can rival the deep grounding in the Chinese classical tradition that Gu Gan combines with an intimate knowledge of Western abstract art – attributes that enable him to create abstract art with meaning.

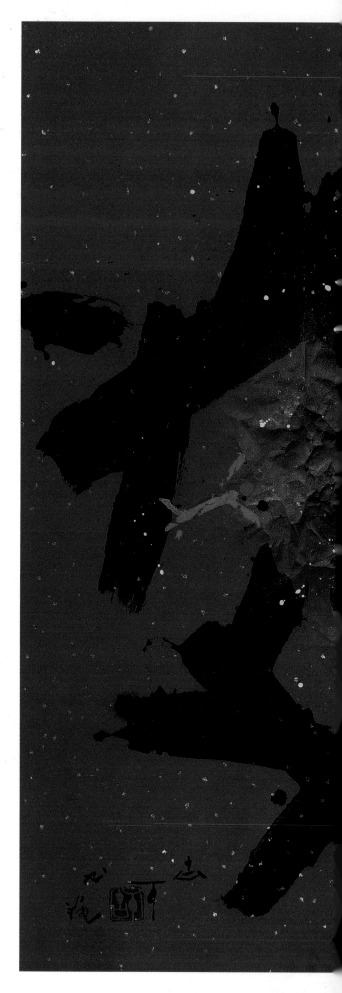

111 *The Age of Red and Gold* completes Gu Gan's trilogy on the theme of modern China, which began with *The Mountains are Breaking Up* (1985), followed by *Opening Up* (1995).